FACES
OF
RIGHT WING
EXTREMISM

by

Kathy Marks

D1534921

BRANDEN PUBLISHING CO.
Boston

SSCCA

© Copyright 1996
by Branden Publishing Company, Inc.

Library of Congress Cataloging-in-Publication Data

Marks, Kathy.
    The faces of right wing extremism / by Kathy Marks.
    p. cm.
    Includes bibliographical references and index.
    ISBN 0-8283-2016-0 (pbk.)
    1. Conservatism--United States.
    2. Political violence--United States.
    3. Radicalism--United States.
      I. Title.
    JC573.2.U6M35 1966
    320.5'.3'.02573--dc20   95-39455
                                                   CIP

BRANDEN PUBLISHING COMPANY, Inc.
17 Station Street
Box 843 Brookline Village
Boston, MA 02147

DEDICATION

This book is dedicated to the real patriots, the hard working honest people who do what is right, people like my grandparents, Amos and Crystabel Johnston and my uncle Orva Johnston who can still climb the mountain. My husband, Bill Marks, is still trying to do what is right and fighting for the right to say what he believes.

ACKNOWLEDGMENTS

This book is the result of several years research which began when I was a graduate student at Southern Illinois University at Carbondale. Dr. Robert Lorinskas was not only my advisor, but thesis chairman, and was of great assistance in learning how to find the needed materials. Dr. James Garofalo, the chairman of the Administration of Justice department, and Dr. Vince Lacey of the Political Science Department, also assisted with my thesis and their ideas and suggestions were further explored.

Jerry Dale, former Pocahontas County, West Virginia, Sheriff, and now Magistrate, provided a great deal of insight into the National Alliance's activities and provided photos of the National Alliance compound. Pam Pritt of the *Pocahontas Times* was very helpful in local information also.

The *Benton Evening News* provided photos of the Klan rally in Benton, Illinois, and these were also appreciated.

Various others have provided information and some would probably prefer not to see their names here. All information has been appreciated, however.

CONTENTS

CHAPTER I

Introduction

I nformation regarding the more radical arm of the right wing movement is not readily available without an extensive search, and much of the information, while available to the public, must be requested from the "watch dog" groups that police the right wing extremists, or from the groups being studied themselves. These groups naturally report facts from their own perspective. Many right wing groups publish their own newsletters, giving their viewpoints (see Appendix L), with these publications often changing names and sometimes operating under more than one name.

Information about specific events is often spread out among a wide field of news media, particularly newspapers and magazines and their reports must be timely and are made on information available at press time, which may change after more information and investigation is done. For instance, the bombing of the federal building in Oklahoma City in 1995 was at first blamed on foreign terrorists and thought to be similar to the earlier bombing of the World Trade Center.

This book is being written to bring the information together and point out the changes that have occurred in the right wing movement in the past quarter of a century. These changes include the populations targeted by right wing violence, the creation of new right wing extremist groups, and changes in the types of violent and criminal activities.

The focus of this book will be these changes in violent right wing groups and the threat that these changes present to targeted minorities and the United States government. Factors examined are the increased violence, changes in the pattern of activities of right wing radicals in the past twenty-five years, and the organization of right wing extremist groups to form conspiracies. The nature of these changes and the dynamics of the persons involved will be examined.

TYPOLOGY

A typology was developed to characterize the individuals involved in right wing extremism. Garson (1976) discussed ideal types that would present a special form of classification that would aid analysis by enabling strong contrasts between the various types. The ideal types could be used as standards against which observed cases could be measured and compared. The ideal types were constructed by the researcher from relevant associated traits.

There is not sufficient information nor statistics to define clear-cut groups, but it is possible to define loose groups that aid in understanding individual motivations and roles. The set of ideal types, or typology, developed is primarily concerned with the attributes of motivation and role within the groups described. Motivation explains how the individuals become involved with radical right wing groups and role explains how the group meets the needs of the individual. This typology gives direction as to how some people become involved with right wing groups, their motivations, and how they come to take action.

GATHERING INFORMATION

Information on right wing extremists, both individuals and groups, can be collected by contacting the various watch dog groups who police right wing radicals. The Anti-Defamation League of B'nai B'rith, the Klanwatch Project of the Southern Poverty Law Center, Political Research Associates, and the Center for Democratic Renewal are the best known of these, with the ADL generally being the more prolific, up to date, and with a broader base of targets than the others.

Other writings about right wing extremists are found in normal research sources, books, magazines, etc. or requested from the groups themselves. There are understandable hazards in this latter activity. These include the threat of a menace from security factions of the groups themselves and scrutiny from the government agencies that police criminal activities of these groups. Law enforcement agencies have many controls about scrutiny of these groups and individuals and federal law often prohibits them gathering information unless there are specific criminal infractions. Information was gathered from publications received at public meetings of various groups and rebuttal information came from well known but less than mainstream publications in some instances, such as *Soldier of Fortune* magazine, in G. Gordon Liddy's case. Information must be gathered and evaluated and needs to come from as wide a base as possible.

Specific information about these groups and individuals is often not available, other than reports of how many are arrested, how much money is stolen in a particular robbery, or how many people they have killed. It is only when that a right wing extremist or group becomes newsworthy, generally with a spectacular event occurring, that information is available from several different **credible** sources at once.

It is the nature of these individuals and organizations to be secretive or deceptive about membership, leadership, structure, and holdings, and much of the information, other than historical information, comes as a result of grand jury testimony, undercover informants, and information gathered by the news media. Empirical data such as membership, structure, and holdings is often lacking from such available information, and an analysis involving conceptualization of these groups and individuals, must use a case study and historical approach.

Government documents pertaining to these groups and individuals are also scarce. There is some information regarding Congressional hearings about the Minutemen, illegal tax protestors, and the Ku Klux Klan, but those hearings were earlier and do not address the changes discussed in this book. There have been other more recent Congressional hearings involving the citizen militia movement, the Branch Davidian incident in Waco, Texas, and the Randy Weaver incident at Ruby Ridge. Transcripts of most of these were not yet available at the time of publication of this book. Intelligence is gathered by government agencies, including the FBI and Internal Revenue Service, but this intelligence information is not usually available to the public.

One 1986 IRS report, *Illegal Tax Protestors Information Handbook*, was not officially released when the media printed information derived from it (Coates, 1987; Anderson and Spears, 1986). This handbook, prepared by Ruth E. Schweizer of the Criminal Investigation Division of the IRS Office of Intelligence, listed organizations "with a propensity for violence," but did not detail why this was the case. It did not contain sufficient intelligence information to be of use in the field and after complaints from several individuals listed in the handbook, including Lois Peterson of the Liberty Lobby, the IRS withdrew the publication and advised that the offices having the document in their possession had been ordered to destroy it (George and Wilcox, 1992). The Liberty Lobby had sold that report in an attempt to show how the right wingers had their rights violated (Coates, 1987). It is this not well organized and often inappropriate use of intelligence about right wing groups that adds fuel to the fire about government interference with individual rights.

Groups are included in this book that have not been linked to any right wing violence or criminal acts. They must be included in order that the general overall picture of right wing extremism be seen.

CHAPTER II

Defining the Right Wing

T he groups and individuals were first examined in reference to their historical background with other right wing groups and individuals and then by differentiating their types of violent actions and the targets of such action. This provided a basis for studying the other factors. The historical background of various right wing groups and individuals, looking at recently created groups, and tracking the various individuals and groups as they evolved in the right wing extremist movement plays an important role in understanding them.

Not all right wing groups are involved in violent acts, although their views may be somewhat extremist in nature. However, because of their extremist views, individuals in the group or with a loose connection to the group, such as someone who has attended meetings and applauded the rhetoric, may go on to perpetrate violent action that is not necessarily supported by the group. Other groups may have some branches that are more extremist and active than others. The militia movement, being an "unorganized" group, has a great deal of variety in members and factions. Some militia groups favor political action, some are neighbors helping neighbors, and some applaud violent militarist action such as the Oklahoma City bombing. Therefore, militias as a whole are discussed later in order to give a more complete picture of the current right wing movement, although many consist of law-abiding American citizens who seek to protect their Constitutional rights lawfully.

After examining the groups and individuals as they evolved in the sphere of right wing activity, other factors were considered. These included the conspiratorial activities among right wing groups, episodes of violence, their desire to establish a white American homeland, use of a theological basis to justify their actions, sophisticated communications systems, and paramilitary and survivalist training to prepare for their version of Armageddon.

DESCRIPTIONS
OF GROUPS AND INDIVIDUALS STUDIED

The similarities and differences in the groups and individuals will also be discussed. Left and right wing groups have both similarities and differences and these will be pointed out. The differences between right wing extremists and other right wing groups and individuals who do not take such radical action will also be discussed. Some right wing groups, such as the John Birch Society, remain within the realms of legal activities, but the John Birch Society is often a breeding ground and starting point for those who then move on to more radical action.

SIMILARITIES IN LEFT AND RIGHT WING

Right wing and left wing terrorists in the United States have many similarities. Their tactics, basic attitudes, and objectives are often similar. They both seek to destroy the American government and the system of constitutional liberties it supports. Both are sworn enemies of "Zionism" and the State of Israel. Both want to replace the American system with their own and subject the majority to their views. While the rightists are more radical and religious bigots and the leftists traditionally support the Communist viewpoint, it is this ideology primarily that separates them (ADL, 1985b).

The concepts became more clearly defined in the twentieth century and "right wing" became associated more with conservatism, religiousness, patriotism, nationalism and racism, while the "left wing" referred to liberalism, secularism, internationalism, collectivism, and egalitarianism (George and Wilcox, 1992). These more clear cut differences make it easier to "label" individuals "right" or "left" but many individuals still have traits that do not lend themselves to such easy description.

Right wing extremists have traits similar to both left and right wing radicals. They have been more violent than their left wing counterparts recently but they have still been able to garner new support and recruits. Like the left, however, they have been motivated in some cases by political causes, which has enlarged their power base (Hoffman, 1986). These causes include such issues as abortion, tax protest, and property rights.

Many of these traits are attributable to both left and right wing extremists and many of the same violent actions have occurred from both. The World Trade Center was bombed by Muslim terrorists and the suspects in the bombing of the Federal Court Building in Oklahoma City appeared to have some association with the Michigan Militia, a right wing militarist and political group. The group denied ties with Timothy McVeigh and the others charged with the violent incident.

The focus of this book will be right wing extremists. The stance traditionally taken by right wing extremists and groups allows them to be readily identified as such. They self-identify with this stance and habitually associate with others of similar identification and interests. Another major point of differentiation of right wing groups is their longer identifiable history and larger numbers than their left wing counterparts.

RIGHT WING EXTREMISTS

Right wing extremists will be defined as those right wing individuals and groups, usually operating at least partially covertly, who commit criminal acts and/or harass, intimidate, or harm other individuals, groups, or the government due to their real or assumed racial/ethnic heritage or their position within the governmental structure of the United States. Having someone to hate is a crucial element to these groups and individuals.

There are certain characteristics generally seen with right wing groups and individuals that help identify them. They usually adhere to a theology with strong religious ties, intense nationalism and patriotism, as they define it, and are against socialist, liberal, and Marxist ideas. They often have well-developed conspiracy theories. Some groups focus on racial and ethnic considerations as a primary part of their ideology. Other groups, such as the

John Birch Society, do not officially include racial prejudice in their ideology (George and Wilcox, 1992).

Finch (1983, p. 8) points out that terms such as extremist or radical are relative. He quotes Robert B. DePugh who founded the Minutemen. "Radical right doesn't mean much. You could call it the American nationalist movement, but not everybody who's part of it is really a nationalist. A lot of people call it the patriotic movement, but you're being generous to call some of these people patriots. This brings us back to 'radical right' and maybe that's as a good a term as any, if you're going to use one."

According to Hoffman (1986), these groups use popular political issues to build a proper base and some of them are well trained, violent, and unpredictable. Coates (1987) stresses that the single most significant characteristic of groups of this nature is their willingness to act, even to lay down their lives for their bigotry. It is this **activism** that separates them from those who merely have conservative political views.

It is often hard to separate legitimate right wing political activities from extremist activities and often people who have previously been involved in lawful activities allow themselves to be drawn into the more extreme and illegal activities. The typology helps explains some of their motivations.

Groups are included in this book that have not been alleged to have committed violent actions. They must be included in order that the overall picture of right wing extremists be viewed.

TARGETS OF VIOLENCE

Organized violence against blacks was widespread after the birth of the Ku Klux Klan in the 1860's. There were periods of depression in the Klan's activities and then periods of upheaval, but when they were active, they have always targeted blacks as victims. The Klans also branched out to have other targets, as will be detailed later.

Right wing extremists often target blacks, whom they see as "mud people" (Bishop, 1988). They also target the Jewish people, citing *The Protocols of the Learned Elders of Zion*, a hoax document that became prominent in arousing hatred against the Jewish in the early 1900's. *The Protocols* cited an international

Jewish conspiracy as the reason for hatred of the Jews (Strong, 1941; Dudman, 1962).

The Protocols, dating from Czarist Russia, were published in Russia and then England, by Sergyei Nilus. *The Protocols* offered the idea that a Jewish conspiracy had been put into motion long ago to destroy the white Gentile race and seize power over the remaining races of the world (Nilus, 1920).

The Protocols has been the most lasting hoax of the conspiracy world. It consists of the minutes of twenty-four purported meetings of anonymous Jewish leaders in their quest to form a program for Jewish conquest and world domination. *The Protocols* helped give focus to anti-Semitism in the extreme right (Finch, 1983). The *Protocols* are still on the reading list of many right wing extremist groups and available from them.

This idea of a Jewish conspiracy to control the world is still prominent among right wing extremists who point to the Federal Reserve as Jewish bankers controlling our monetary system. They point to this as further evidence that there is a conspiracy to rule the world in referring to the United Nations taking over the United States for a "one world government."

This "one world government" is a central concern of many right wing groups and has continued with the recent organization of militias in many states. Militias, which vary widely from state to state, and sometimes bill themselves as "patriot organizations," distribute literature and other materials informing the public about the goals and evils of one world government.

Formal ideologies often contain elements of a conspiracy theory. This includes an explanation of why one group consists of victims and the others are victimizers. This theory often explains how the victimizers are doing evil things to their victims and a course of action to right the wrongs (George and Wilcox, 1992).

Organized violent actions also began being directed toward the government, beginning in the 1960's with the Minutemen and growing in strength, quantity, and violence in the 1980's. The 1990's have already seen greater violence than has ever been seen on American soil by terrorists with the bombing of the Federal Court Building in Oklahoma City in April 1995. Recent trends have also shown an effort to unify hate groups and form coalitions.

WHY IS THIS INFORMATION IMPORTANT?

Law enforcement officials, especially those at the federal level, have appeared to underestimate or be unaware of the dangers posed by right wing extremists and groups. The federal government has been widely criticized for their actions in the recent disasters involving actions against Gordon Kahl, Randy Weaver, David Koresh, and others. Kahl, Weaver, and Koresh have become martyrs for the right wing cause. Better planning, intelligence gathering, and cooperation among the various law enforcement agencies might have helped prevent some of the violent episodes and tragedies detailed in this book.

Exploring the conspiratorial nature of right wing radicals and studying their capacity for violence may provide needed information to law enforcement agencies that cross their paths. There needs to be a recognition that the United States is not immune to violence from political extremists within its own borders.

For many years, United States citizens saw bombings and other civil disorder on foreign soil but never expected such crises to come to rural America. The disaster and many deaths at Oklahoma City brought this home to government officials and the general public overnight.

The United States government has historically not taken right wing extremist groups seriously. For instance, when the House Un-American Activities Committee announced that it was going after Communists on a grand scale, it refused to look at the Ku Klux Klan, with one Congressman calling the Klan "as American as illegal whiskey selling" (Wade, 1987, p. 287). There have been Congressional hearings involving Nazis and illegal tax protestors, but the previous hearings did not target the changes in the right wing radical movement. Such hearings have only recently come about and have centered more on weapons issues, intelligence gathering, and allegations of improper action and misconduct of federal law enforcement people in standoff situations, such as the Branch Davidian assault and Randy Weaver incident. June 1995 Congressional hearings involving the citizen militias were not yet available in transcript at this book's completion, nor were transcripts of the Weaver and Branch Davidian hearings.

According to Hoffman (1986), there is a natural inclination to dismiss the right wing extremists as uneducated country bumpkins, hotheads or mentally unstable alarmists. However, these individuals and groups have demonstrated they are serious in their beliefs, dedicated to their causes, and are willing to use violence in pursuit of their goals. Authorities are now beginning to realize just how far the radical right will go and the technological capabilities they possess.

Right wing extremists are not the isolated, technically unsophisticated pipe bomb manufacturers who dominated most of the terrorist activity in the United States previously. They are well trained in the use of arms and explosives, skilled armorers and bomb makers, and they are adept in guerilla warfare techniques and outdoor survival. They are violent, mercurial and unpredictable, factors which make an analysis of their behavior difficult (Hoffman, 1986). They have access to nearly any type of sophisticated weaponry and communications equipment. This comes from the same government they seek to overthrow, and is stolen or black marketed from military storage facilities. There have been criminal prosecutions of military personnel who have stolen and black marketed materials to right wing groups. They have testified about the lax security on military bases.

There are two major concerns about right wing extremists. They are very well armed and erratic, and they already possess an active domestic network of terrorists who pose a serious threat of political assassination, racial violence, and other assorted types of armed mayhem. Secondly, these groups, with an alarming willingness to **act**, have re-invigorated the far right movement to a height it had never reached before (Coates, 1987). The new militia movement and the skinhead movement, both of which have ties to many previous right wing organizations, have gained popular support to a greater extent than any group in recent years.

This willingness to act has changed the dynamics of the groups and individuals involved. Never before in this century has a right wing extremist group tried to overthrow the U. S. government, and the extremists have announced their intentions of taking this action.

Hubert Williams (Williams, 1986), while President of the Police Foundation in Washington, D.C., discussed right wing groups in *Terrorism* magazine. He found that information about right wing groups was not included in most literature about terrorist groups in America. He discussed their methods as violent, their goals as political and oppressive, and as them having an extensive arsenal of arms and sophisticated weaponry. He believed this group of community based white supremacists was large and growing and more dangerous to the fabric of our society than foreign terrorists.

The changes in the right wing in the past quarter of a century parallel the changes in the fabric of our society. The American public is angry about taxes, angry about having to lock their doors to keep out their neighbors, angry about crooked and greedy politicians, angry about drug abuse, and they are beginning to express their anger in many ways, from the political process, to joining citizen militias, lobbying against gun control, and blowing up the federal building in Oklahoma City.

It is important that when these groups and individuals are scrutinized, that it is done because they are committing criminal acts and violating the rights of others, not because they are exercising their constitutional rights in a manner not approved by the majority. Often in the past, the reaction by the United States government has been to overreact and look for "reds" hiding under every rock. The mood of the American public may not tolerate such invasions of their rights at this point in American history. That is why it is important that officials understand where these groups and individuals are coming from and where they are going.

CHAPTER III

Typology
of Right Wing Extremists

The individuals involved in the groups discussed can better be understood by looking at their motivation and their needs and how their needs are met by membership in the groups. This typology can be of assistance in defining the right wing extremists being examined from the rest of the right wing movement, who may be lawfully exercising their constitutional rights and freedoms.

Due to the nature of these individuals and groups, there is little aggregate empirical data for analysis. Therefore, a historical and conceptual viewpoint is more appropriate for studying their dynamics (Garson, 1976).

The following typology was developed. The traits examined in reference to particular individuals were the roles they played within the organization and how it met their needs, and their motivations, or reasons for being involved with the groups. Six types were defined: career extremist, dedicated follower, the dispossessed, hard core criminals, thrill seekers, and the delusional personality.

CAREER EXTREMISTS

Career extremists are those charismatic leaders who are "salesmen" for the movement. They have generally been involved in right wing activities most of their adult lives and at some point this has become their life's work. They often do not have an outside job, having retired or given up their previous career. They are supported by their organization, or often have used their retirement or savings to create this same organization. These individuals seek out the followers listed, each type of individual for different reasons. The career extremists recruit these individuals, building a power base and organization. They instill in these followers the faith and devotion needed to keep the "cause" alive.

They often use religion to justify their thoughts and actions. They are different from left wing leaders in that they are generally more isolated from violent acts and criminal prosecutions. Some of the career extremists discussed are Richard Butler, Robert Miles, and William Potter Gale.

DEDICATED FOLLOWERS

Dedicated followers are the faithful right wing extremists who have always been a part of one group or another but may have a life outside the group, at least in the beginning of their involvement. However, it is these people who may be very content to live within the perimeters of the group, within that group's own home compound.

These individuals may be poorly educated and not worldly. It is easy for them to accept that a conspiracy of Jewish or black people has taken from them what is rightly theirs, keeping them as a downtrodden underculture, and their only recourse is armed revolution to take back what is rightfully theirs.

This group of people is very useful to the leader of the group because of their blind devotion and single-minded dedication to the "cause." They are able to be recognized as part of a group, a place for them to "belong." These followers are sometimes among the most dangerous extremists because they blindly place their faith in the charismatic leader and their cause and are willing to commit criminal acts, even murder, in the name of the faith. They often have distorted religious convictions that bolster their faith in the group. The group fulfills their need to be recognized and belong and gives them a "cause." People such as Jean Craig, who became involved with the Order, typify this category.

Zielenziger (1986, p. 1) describes this phenomenon in discussing Pastor Thom Robb, National Chaplain of the Knights of the

Ku Klux Klan, and leader of the Church of Jesus Christ in Harrison, Arizona, an Identity church. Robb indicated, "A strictly political movement can be bought off or sabotaged. You can't stop a religious movement the way you can a political one because people believe they are being led by God."

THE DISPOSSESSED

The dispossessed are those generally honest, hard working Americans who have fallen upon hard times or have come to believe their government is no longer representing them. They see their hard times as being caused by governmental actions and by minorities taking what they believe should be theirs. They believe that their rights have been trampled and they are no longer being able to exercise their constitutional rights as they see them due to a government that has grown too large and too nosy.

The Midwest farmers are a prime example of those who have fallen on hard times. It is easy to convince them that a conspiracy exists that has caused their hardship (Corcoran, 1990). Dixon Terry, Chairman of the Iowa Farm Unit Coalition explained it, "Farmers are victims of the hate propaganda and phony schemes of a surprisingly strong, organized right wing element" (Hoffman, 1986, p. 8).

The dispossessed farmers see the government as giving handouts to those whom they see as undeserving and that same government taking from them what they have given their life to preserve - the family farm. They join groups such as the Posse Comitatus and hell hath no fury like a man dispossessed of his heritage and ability to support his family like a man, as he sees it. In the 1970's, the Posse and Christian Identity groups traced the roots of the farmers' problems to racist and anti-Semitic reasons (Corcoran, 1990).

Rural radical right organizers have built the infrastructure of a racist and anti-Semitic movement upon the despair and frustrations of these family farmers. These crises in rural communities have led to the groups stockpiling weapons and issuing shrill calls to prepare for battle (Smith, 1987). It was this same shrill call that Gordon Kahl heard and answered. The role played by this type of individual is often that of a martyr or a man who has been wronged by the system.

More recently, the dispossessed group has grown greatly, at least those who see themselves dispossessed of what they believe should be theirs under the American constitutional system. More and more mainstream Americans are becoming more verbal and organizing against a government they see as unresponsive to their needs. The dispossessed individual is also seen in the more militant of the recently organized "unorganized state militias," although many other mainstream Americans who have not become so embittered but see them as "patriotic" also join. This dispossessed group has grown and continues to grow. The extent of their action may be determined by the government's responses their grievances.

Tim McVeigh, who is accused in the Oklahoma City bombing, was reportedly a soldier's soldier until he became disillusioned after not making the grade to Special Forces. He became embittered and involved in right wing activities. He, along with others, is accused of perpetrating the largest mass killing in U. S. history, including many children and infants in America's Kids Day Care, located in the bombed federal building. He still awaits trial and has pled "not guilty."

HARD CORE CRIMINALS

The hard core criminal element consists of those persons who would be committing criminal acts no matter where they are nesting or with whom. These individuals move from group to group, generally gravitating to the more violent and profitable branches. Their usual motivation is from a desire for profit, and/or power. The role they play is often that of an enforcer or participant in criminal activities, such as robberies or murders.

Theology is less important than money and perks. They find their niche in a group that applauds their criminal prowess and expertise and may even recruit them for these qualities. Some right wing extremist groups recruit within the prison systems and have spots awaiting their recruits upon their release. Many of the zealous leaders and members of lawless extremist groups are in prison or have served time, and this has added to the recruitment process within the prison wall.

THRILL SEEKERS

Thrill seekers are among the most erratic, unpredictable and dangerous of the individuals being studied. They are generally younger than the other types of people on the edge of violence. They commit criminal acts frequently, but do not typify the hard core criminal element because they are not primarily profit motivated. They are motivated instead by the desire to get their kicks and have power over someone.

The thrill seekers commit violent acts for the sake of violence, for the thrill they get from hurting someone or intimidating someone weaker than themselves. They are often indiscriminate in their choices of targets and are easily led and influenced by the charismatic leaders of the groups, especially when the leader is calling for violence.

They often travel in "packs" and find it easier to bully their targets in that manner. This type individual is used by the leaders as "muscle" to get their point across and cause fear and consternation because of this individual's unpredictability. This type of person has revitalized the right wing movement because they have no limits on the acts they will commit. This type of individual gets his kicks from violence and is not aversive to committing more violent acts for which he gets approval. Individuals involved in "skin head" groups and individuals who act as enforcers and "muscle" for other groups fit in this type of individual's category.

THE DELUSIONAL PERSONALITIES

These individuals are the rarest of those seen in connection with extremism, but their level of violence, extreme range of violent behavior, and aberrations enhance their level of risk because of their unpredictability. These are people who latch onto an idea that appeals to them and then add their own perverted twists. They see reality from their own perspective and get messages from God or from outer space or from animals in the field, and they march to a different drummer.

The right wing movement has attracted some of these individuals and may not approve of their actions in some cases, but clearly has exerted an influence over them. These individuals often set up their own compound over which they have total power and control.

Their motivations come from no logical source but from some delusional source within themselves, although they have been influenced in their ideology by right wing extremist ideas. They generally have no major role in the movement itself. They do have a self-created role because they are acting for a "cause" they have adopted, but the movement cannot show approval for their actions without itself being seen as an aberration.

At least one of these individuals has come to play a major role in the right wing extremist movement, after his death. Sometimes right wing extremists do approve of the actions of irrational people, when it suits their purposes. Some of these individuals, such as David Koresh, are applauded by the right wing movement and seen as martyrs because they were seeking religious freedom. Because of the final ending of the Branch Davidian incident, right wing extremists point to it as improper action by federal law enforcement officials and allege that the government is responsible for the deaths of those who perished at the Branch Davidian. Just as any other group using propaganda for their own purposes, those who applaud David Koresh have ignored the reports of child abuse and abuse of other members of the Branch Davidian community by David Koresh. While the Waco incident was complicated by many errors of judgment, that does not change what David Koresh was doing or how he was invading the rights of others, and taking advantage of children, in the name of religious freedom.

The Branch Davidian incident should be carefully scrutinized in order that it should not recur. However, playing David Koresh as a hero and martyr instead of a madman who has to take his own responsibility for the deaths there is not a responsible route to encourage the right to pursue religious freedoms.

CHAPTER IV

Historical Review of Right Wing Groups

Considerable information exists in the form of historical literature about broad topics, such as the Ku Klux Klan. There is also literature discussing the early neo-Nazi groups and the Minutemen of the 1960's. The literature base regarding the more recent groups and individuals beginning in the 1970's and studying the interrelations of these groups and their members is slim and comes from a small group of sources in most instances. As recently as the early 1990's, new interest has developed because of some of the more newsworthy events discussed in this book.

The focus of this book, after dealing with the groups and individuals in a historical context and study of the evolution of the newer groups, will be the changes seen beginning with the 1970's and continuing to 1995. Earlier groups must be discussed to give a background to understand the current groups. Some of the groups discussed are not involved in criminal activities, but must be included to better understand the interrelationships of the groups and individuals who are being studied.

Problems in studying these groups include not only the scarcity of materials, but the secretive nature of the groups. Groups such as the Posse Comitatus are urged by their leaders to join other groups and keep their connections with the Posse secret.

ETHICAL AND LEGAL QUESTIONS

There are ethical and legal questions in studying groups and individuals who are engaged in what may be legal political protests against the United States government and against certain other targeted citizens. Most political protests involve activities that are legal. There are limits on what state and federal governments can do as far as surveillance and police actions and the U. S. Supreme Court has in the past defined what is permissible from radical groups and individuals in their attacks on the American way. The following are some of the landmark cases involving political protest against the United States government and individual rights.

SCHENCK V. UNITED STATES (1919)

The United States Supreme Court has taken notice of these legal questions. *Schenck v. United States* (1919) was the first of the precedent setting cases involving groups whose political ideas might clash with compelling state interests. It was later mostly overridden, but this was the case where the "clear and present danger" clause came into being, with Congress having the power to punish violations of this clause. Schenck, General Secretary of the Socialist Party, was prosecuted for violations of the 1917 Espionage Act, which made it a federal crime to interfere with military recruitment or adversely affect military morale. The **intent** of the speaker was a crucial element of the offense. Schenck and his colleagues distributed leaflets opposing the military draft and the United States entering World War I. Schenck was convicted of conspiring to obstruct the draft and other violations of the Act. His attorneys argued that the Act violated the First Amendment by punishing free speech and that Schenck was acting within his rights of freedom of speech.

The Court affirmed the judgment, with Justice Holmes delivering the unanimous opinion of the Court:

> The character of every act depends upon the circumstances in which it is done. . . The most stringent protection of free speech would not protect a man in falsely shouting fire in a theater and causing a panic. . . The question in every case is whether words used are used in such circumstances and are of such a nature that they create a clear and present danger that

they will bring about the substantive evils that Congress has a right to prevent (Saye, 1975, p. 258; Goldman, 1991, p. 424).

GITLOW V. NEW YORK (1925)

Gitlow v. New York (1925) was a case involving Gitlow, a member of the Left Wing of the Socialist party, who advocated "revolutionary mass action" to overthrow the government by force, violence, or other unlawful means. He was convicted of violating the New York State Anarchy Act of 1902 because of his actions in having a Manifesto published to this end. The issue was whether the New York statute deprived Gitlow of his liberties of speech and press without due process in violation of the Fourteenth Amendment.

The Court took this opportunity to further refine the "clear and present danger" idea. The court held that the statute was not unconstitutional and had been applied in a constitutionally acceptable manner. Justice Sanford delivered the opinion of the Court:

> It is a fundamental principle, long established, that the freedom of speech and the press which is secured by the Constitution, does not confer an absolute right to speak or publish, without responsibility, whatever one may choose. . . That a State in the exercise of its police power may punish those who abuse this freedom by utterances inimical to the public welfare, tending to corrupt public morals, incite to crime, or disturb the public peace, is not open to question. . . (Goldman, 1991, p. 426; Saye, 1975, p. 259).

WHITNEY V. CALIFORNIA (1927)

Justice Brandeis wrote the majority opinion in *Whitney v. California,* rather than dissenting, to exert his influence on the majority to protect the principles of freedom of speech and assembly. Miss Whitney was convicted of organizing the Communist Labor Party of California, being a member and assembling with it, thus constituting a crime because the party was formed to teach criminal syndicalism. The statute restricted the right of free speech and assembly previously existing. The issue was whether the statute, as applied in the case, denied Miss Whitney the liberty guaranteed by the Fourteenth Amendment.

Justice Brandeis put more polish on the "clear and present danger" clause and also more restrictions. He stated that *Schenck v. United States* had already established that rights of free speech and assembly, while fundamental, were not absolute and their exercise could be restricted, but that a valid restriction would not exist unless such speech would produce, or was intended to produce, a clear and imminent danger of some substantive evil which the state could constitutionally act upon (Goldman, 1991, 428).

Brandeis clarified the new position:

> To justify suppression of free speech there must be reasonable ground to fear that serious evil will result if free speech is practiced. There must be reasonable ground to believe that the danger apprehended is imminent. There must be reasonable ground to believe that the evil to be prevented is a serious one (Goldman, 1991, 429).

The Court held that merely being a member of a political party and advocating a revolution at some future date was not in violation of the Fourteenth Amendment but held that in Miss Whitney's case, other factors existed that tended to establish the conspiracy to commit serious crimes and upheld the judgment of the state court against her.

Whitney v. California could be of importance to activities of extremist right wing groups when one considers that they are members of political groups and are essentially advocating a revolution at some future time.

BRYANT V. ZIMMERMAN (1928)

Bryant v. Zimmerman (1928) was the first of these cases involving right wing extremist groups. It is still used in considering precedent on decisions involving freedom of association, the issue in the case being whether a state statute requiring filing of membership lists violated the right of freedom of association. The U. S. Supreme Court upheld a New York statute requiring any unincorporated association which demanded an oath as a condition of membership to file membership papers. The holding was in application of the statute to the Ku Klux Klan. The Court emphasized that the "nature of the Klan's activities, involving acts of unlawful intimidation and violence, which the Court assumed was before the state legislature when it enacted the statue and of which the Court itself took judicial notice" (Saye, 1975, p. 295), persuaded it to make this finding.

Court findings have traditionally provided that merely verbally expressing one's political views or abstract teachings is acceptable, but when violent action is present or is being encouraged, that it is a lawful and appropriate area for regulation. For instance, in *Noto v. United States (1961)*, the Court stated, "the mere abstract teaching... of the moral propriety or even moral necessity for a resort to force and violence is not the same as preparing a group for violent action and steeling it to such action" (Goldman, 1991, p. 441). The above legal position probably supports government surveillance methods and suggests that the matter needs to be better defined to determine what is generally constitutionally acceptable in surveillance.

NAACP V. ALABAMA (1958)

The Supreme Court showed that the circumstances involved would decide how the rules should be applied. In *NAACP v. Alabama* (1958), the Court reviewed an Alabama statute that had been applied to the NAACP requiring that membership lists be filed for foreign corporations and trying to force the NAACP to comply.

The NAACP had always thought itself exempt and had never filed in the decades since the statute had been in effect. The issue was whether the state's interest in compelling the membership list was sufficient to justify abridging the rights of freedom of association.

The U. S. Supreme Court held that Alabama had fallen short "of showing a controlling justification for the deterrent effect on the free enjoyment of the right to associate, which disclosure of membership lists is likely to have" (Goldman, 1991, p. 294; Saye, 1975, p. 293).

BRANDENBURG V. OHIO (1969)

Brandenburg v. Ohio (1969) pointed out that political freedom, to mean anything, must apply not only to those whom society supports, but also those whom parts of society may detest. The case applied the Ohio Criminal Syndicalism statute to the Ku Klux Klan. This statute disallowed advocating terrorism as a means of accomplishing political reform and assembling a group to teach or advocate criminal syndicalism. The appellant challenged the constitutionality of the statute under the First and Fourteenth Amendments.

Lower courts affirmed the conviction or dismissed the appeal. The U. S. Supreme Court reversed the conviction and held that decisions had fashioned the principle that the constitutional guarantees of freedom of speech and free press do not permit a State to forbid or proscribe advocacy of the use of force or of law violation except where such advocacy is directed to inciting or producing imminent lawless action and is likely to incite or produce such action (Goldman, 1991; Rotunda, 1987).

This decision relied on the earlier discussed decision, *Noto v. United States (1961)* that stated "the mere abstract teaching. . . of the moral propriety or even moral necessity for a resort to force and violence is not the same as preparing a group for violent action and steeling it to such action" (Goldman, 1991, p. 441).

MURPHY V. MISSOURI
DEPARTMENT OF CORRECTIONS (1985)

Court findings have also dealt with inmates' claims to religious freedoms. *Murphy v. Missouri Department of Corrections (1985)* involved a challenge by an inmate that the institution's policy of withholding inflammatory literature sent by the Aryan Nations and other groups violated his rights. The U. S. District Court held against the inmate on their free speech claim, holding that the prison's literature ban was justified by a substantial government interest in safeguarding prison security (ADL, 1986).

This case was important because of the great effort that has been made to recruit prisoners for prison white racist groups and involve them in groups such as the Aryan Nations upon their release from prison. This ruling approved of the prison's policy in not allowing inflammatory literature that would cause security problems between the white right wing prison groups and other minority groups.

MCCABE V. ARAVE (1986)

Leaders of right wing extremist prison ministries see prisoners who share their views as POW's in a war between the government and the far right. These leaders have sought to send white supremacy literature, questioning the rights of the federal government to imprison them and praising groups and individuals who became martyrs for the right wing, such as Bob Mathews and the Order.

McCabe v. Arave (1986) addressed one such issue. The United States District Court in Idaho dismissed a complaint filed by Melvin McCabe and Mark Madsden, members of the Church of Jesus Christ Christian (Aryan Nations), alleging that prison officials violated their free exercise rights by denying permission to conduct worship services, hold study groups, meet with church officials, and perform other actions normally associated with religious worship. The district court held that the Church of Jesus Christ Christian and the Aryan Nations were "alter-egos" and "two halves of one theo-political organization" and that the inmates' free exercise rights were subject to appropriate restrictions by the prison which are reasonable and necessary to preserve order and security (ADL, 1986).

Basically what this did was support the earlier decision in *Murphy v. Missouri Department of Corrections* that allows prison officials to monitor and disallow certain materials to come into the prison that might cause security problems between inmates that would endanger guards and security within the prison. This case prevented the various organizations from simply sending the same materials from their "religious" organization, instead of their "political" one.

CIVIL RIGHTS VIOLATIONS?

During the 1960's and the civil rights movement, conflict between local law enforcement and judicial systems, and federal prosecutors and law enforcement officers developed. Cases involving black victims and white defendants were rarely prosecuted, and federal authorities sought a way to prosecute cases where the death of black victims came about because of right wing extremists, generally the Ku Klux Klans.

There were questions with criminal prosecutions about who had jurisdiction and whether violations of civil rights existed when individuals were murdered because of their race or if this should be handled through state criminal courts on murder charges. Three civil rights workers were murdered in Mississippi in 1964. This attracted national attention and has continued to do so in books and movies, such as the movie *Mississippi Burning.*

THE FAMOUS CIVIL RIGHTS MURDERS

Michael Schwerner, a bearded white northern Jewish civil rights worker had, since 1963, been assisting southern blacks in Meridian, Mississippi. The Council of Federations Organizations (COFO) was formed in Mississippi in 1964 to unite both blacks and supporting whites. They had put out a call for help in registering voters. Volunteers were warned they might be injured or killed and white terrorists, often the Knights of the Ku Klux Klan, burned and bombed Mississippi churches used as COFO meeting places.

When the Mount Zion Church in Neshoba County, Mississippi, was burned on June 16, 1964, Schwerner and two friends, Andrew Goodman, a twenty-year-old white New York student who arrived the day before, and James Chaney, a twenty-one-year-old black plasterer from Meridian, went to investigate.

The three left for the church on June 21st and Deputy Sheriff Cecil Price stopped them for speeding near Philadelphia, Mississippi. He held them in jail for more than six hours, releasing them about 10:30 p.m. when Chaney posed $20 bond. The three then reportedly left for Meridian. The FBI was called when the men failed to return.

Two days later, the station wagon they were riding in was found burned near Philadelphia, Mississippi. The FBI searched, along with sailors from the Meridian Naval Air Station who had been ordered into the search by President Lyndon B. Johnson. Acting on a tip, the FBI recovered the bodies under a recently built earth dam near Philadelphia on August 4, 1964, all three having been shot to death.

The FBI continued its investigation and convened a federal grand jury to hear evidence on civil rights violations. They could not investigate the murders as murder because murder is not a federal crime. The FBI eventually arrested nineteen men, including Neshoba County Sheriff Lawrence Rainey, Deputy Sheriff Price, a policeman, a minister, and a variety of others, most of them reportedly Klan members. The men were charged with civil rights violations (Ginger, 1973).

Evidence proved that the three civil rights workers had been shot to death by the Klansmen with the help of the local officials. No state murder charges were ever brought against any of the men. Although the murders could be proven, the maximum sentence was ten years in prison under federal law for "conspiracy to violate civil rights" (Tucker, 1991, p. 188).

New evidence kept coming in and the grand jury was reconvened. Indictments were handed down and the indictments stated that the defendants had acted "under color of law" to deprive the men of life and liberty without due process of law, in violation of the Fourteenth Amendment.

Federal District Judge William A. Cox was a confirmed segregationist and there were objections to him sitting on the case. In February 1965, he ruled against the Justice Department and dismissed all the indictments except the three law enforcement officers, saying the others had not acted "under color of law." He noted that murder was not a federal offense unless committed on federal property and the government could not use a civil rights statute to prosecute for murder.

Justice Abe Fortas of the U. S. Supreme Court delivered the unanimous decision of the Court in March 1966 and held that it was an error to dismiss the indictments and sent the case back for trial, relying on the Fourteenth Amendment--that no State shall deprive any person of life or liberty without due process of law. This decision is considered a landmark because it said that the old law meant what it said and was going to be enforced.

Before the trial was held, Judge Cox again dismissed the indictments, alleging an improperly selected grand jury. A new grand jury was selected and again indictments were returned. Several more holdups occurred from Judge Cox's various rulings but the trial was finally held in October 1967. Seven of the defendants were found guilty, eight not guilty, and three had a deadlocked jury. This was the first time a white jury had found white men guilty in a civil rights slaying in Mississippi. Deputy Sheriff Price and Klan Imperial Wizard Bowers were among those convicted. The Sheriff was acquitted and left the state. Bowers and another defendant received the maximum ten years, with Price and another man receiving six years each. The State of Mississippi never filed murder charges against anyone in the three deaths (Ginger, 1973).

This slaying of three young civil rights workers is much more important than a reading of it might imply. For years, the southern Klans had been immune to prosecution because local prosecutors refused to file charges and local juries would not have convicted them anyhow. This case received such nationwide attention and such scrutiny that "doing what was right" became the only option left. With this landmark case, federal prosecutors had found a way to prosecute such cases successfully. This massive public scrutiny may have also persuaded some local prosecutors to file local charges in some cases.

RIGHT WING GROUPS SAW GROWTH

Lawless conduct by both right wing and left wing groups have resulted in prison convictions for Ku Klux Klan leaders, neo-Nazis, and the Order on the right and Black Liberation Army and the Weather Underground on the left. Both right and left wing groups have targeted prison recruitment and see their members in jail as "prisoners of war" (ADL, 1986).

The right wing movement is targeted in this book because of a revival in the 1970's, sparked by things such as the Klan exploiting racial issues, such as busing. This revival was fueled by other factors plaguing Americans, such as rising inflation, the Vietnam war, an energy crisis, and a backlash against the strong counterculture of the times. It was during the mid to late 1970's that several new hate groups arose, including the Aryan Nations, Christian Patriots Defense League, the Covenant, Sword, and the Arm of the Lord (CSA), and some newer Klan and neo-Nazi factions (Suall and Lowe, 1987).

The rise in activity continued through the 1980's and beyond. In the early 1990's, the Branch Davidians assault in Waco, Texas, the Randy Weaver incident, and the blossoming citizen militias added fuel to the fire. The public saw scandal after scandal involving elected government officials and saw their elected officials passing legislation that did not reflect their views. The Oklahoma City bombing brought the right wing movement into the public eye more than it had ever been before.

This upsurge is the basis for this book. Even after the major flood of violence slowed, there was a renewed emphasis on colonizing the northwest among some of the most violence-prone white supremacist organizations (CDR, 1988). Midwest farmers and those advocating states' rights and the authority of the county as the only lawful authority, such as the Posse Comitatus, came into public view.

In the mid 1990's, the state militias which had organized began to make themselves known and to get involved in political causes and elections. Some of the more radical people who had claimed to be members became involved in criminal activities, such as the federal building bombing in Oklahoma City on April 19, 1995.

Some of the events that center around the most newsworthy of the groups and individuals of this era showed that the activities were different than those seen with earlier extremist groups and individuals. These included the Order, and later, those accused of bombing the federal court building in Oklahoma City. The Order was involved in the initial stage of a revolution aimed at overthrowing the United States government and the bombing appeared to target various government offices also. The events centered around the Order made up the first attempt in this century by right wing extremists to launch a violent revolution against the United States government (ADL, 1985b).

Although right wing groups have a long history, including the Klans and then Nazi-type organizations such as the Silver Shirts of the 1930's (Strong, 1941), there were fewer and less varied groups than those in current existence. The John Birch Society and the Minutemen, the best known groups of the 1950's and 1960's, were the forefathers of many of the individual radicals and groups that exist today (Epstein and Forster, 1967).

JOHN BIRCH SOCIETY

John Birch was a Baptist missionary executed in China and in 1958 he was elevated to martyrdom by Robert Welch who named the group after him. He was killed by Chinese Communists after World War II ended. Welch believed that Birch's character personified the traits and ideals he wanted to be symbolized by the John Birch Society (George and Wilcox, 1992).

Robert H. W. Welch, Jr., was a retired candy manufacturer and was "grand wazir" of the group until his death in 1985. Many Americans have long considered the John Birch Society to be part of the extremist fringe (George and Wilcox, 1992), whether or not they are involved in criminal acts. It was intended to be a grassroots American campaign to fight communism (Flynn and Gerhardt, 1989). It was begun as a patriotic American effort to root out Communism. In the 1960's, the Society was described as the "spearhead of the radical right" (Epstein and Forster, 1967, p. 3).

Welch withdrew from his business in 1957 to contemplate the Communist conspiracy full-time. He summoned friends together in December 1958 to talk about the international Communist conspiracy. It was then that he and his friends founded the John Birch Society, to be a revolutionary and religious organization with people of all religions. It would be devoted to fighting Communism (George and Wilcox, 1992).

The John Birch Society periodically admonishes its membership for anti-Semitic traits but is noted to have a tendency to attract anti-Semites (Epstein and Forster, 1967). The Birchers are not associated with violent acts, but many present day radicals who have committed violent acts began with the John Birch Society (see Appendix A), men such as Robert Mathews and

Richard Scutari of the Order (Martinez and Guinther, 1988). Some right wing extremists, such as J. B. Stoner, have been infuriated with the John Birch Society and Robert Welch for years because the organization refused to take a racist stance. There are racists within the Society but they are not allowed to publicly advertise as such (Finch, 1983).

The John Birch Society is still in full swing. They have candidates running for various political offices, including Congressional offices. They have not been tied to criminal acts but their members have often gone on to bigger and better things. When Welch died in January 1985, the organization suffered setbacks and loss of members (George and Wilcox, 1992), but is still a viable organization within the right wing.

THE MINUTEMEN

The Minutemen were one of the most militant right wing groups until recent years, and the more militant newer groups have many organizational similarities. There is no evidence to document their current existence.

The Minutemen created a great deal of fear and apprehension during the 1960's. They tried to attract attention and send panic throughout their enemies' ranks. The Minutemen showed what one man could do using the media for attention and also showed the extent of government infiltration into extremist organizations (George and Wilcox, 1992).

Robert Bolivar DePugh began the Minutemen in Independence, Missouri, in 1960. At the time, he was a chemist from Norborne, Missouri. He was a former member of the John Birch Society who was dropped because of his underground armed guerilla activities (ADL, 1988a).

The Minutemen became one of the most feared right wing movements of its time because of the group's violence and its defiance of law enforcement agencies and governmental officials. They were well organized, with weaponry, a secret cell structure, and a united front (Flynn and Gerhardt, 1989). The group threatened their perceived enemies, and *On Target*, their publication, named those they saw as traitors (ADL, 1988a).

The group reportedly started after a hunting party of DePugh's discussed that, in a Communist invasion of the United States, parties such as theirs could turn into guerilla bands and fight from the hills. This eventually led to a movement, familiar with guerilla tactics, paramilitary training and maneuvers, and stockpiling weapons and ammunition. This, at least, was the official story in the Minutemen publications. It may actually have been the literature from other groups that gave them their impetus (George and Wilcox, 1992).

DePugh claimed 25,000 members for this super-secret league of guerillas. They had guns, pistols, mortars, bazookas, and grenades. There were bands of 5-15 Minutemen who conducted field exercises and classes. They had a security system including coded messages, mail drops and chemical treatment of materials so they would destroy themselves if the papers fell into enemy hands (Dudman, 1962).

Minutemen were told to find the communist enemy within, to which end DePugh built an enemy file on 65,000 individuals and named fifteen hundred persons whom he saw as traitors who would be targeted for assassination in the event of a coup. Minutemen were encouraged to join other right wing groups such as the John Birch Society, which also looked for the Communist enemy within. DePugh's group was an umbrella organization for most of the nation's paramilitary groups at that time (Ridgeway, 1990).

Bands of five to fifteen men conducted field exercises and used a security system with coded messages, mail drops, and chemically treated documents that would self-destruct if they fell into enemy hands (Dudman, 1962). They prepared for a last ditch defense against communist takeover with secret numbered networks, survivalist camps for explosives and weapons training, and intelligence files on their enemies (Flynn and Gerhardt, 1989).

John George and Laird Wilcox (1992) in a detailed study of DePugh, indicate that the Minutemen was one of the most thoroughly infiltrated domestic far right groups by the government and when one of the members got into trouble with the police, he traded information for more lenient treatment. They also dispute the numbers given by DePugh, saying he gave huge distorted figures when the number of actual active Minutemen was probably in the hundreds. The Secret Army Organization from southern California also had tenuous ties to the Minutemen, but was also infiltrated by an informant-agent working for the FBI and ATF.

In 1969, DePugh was convicted and sentenced to an eleven-year term in federal prison for firearms laws' violations, bond jumping and violation of federal gun control laws (ADL, 1988a). He later led an ultra-conservative umbrella group called the "Committee of 10 Million" (Flynn and Gerhardt, 1989). He sought to unite ten million patriots to change the American system of government. This group was not very successful (ADL, 1988a). Because of DePugh's longtime devotion to the right wing movement and his continued leadership role and recruitment of followers, he is typical of the "career extremist" developed in the typology.

DePugh also started his own third party political group, called the Patriotic Party, closely connected to the Minutemen, which did not achieve the prominence he sought (Epstein and Forster, 1967). Right wing extremist groups often consist of various branches used to further particular interests of that group, such as a political arm for lobbying and putting forth candidates and a religious branch for acquiring tax exempt status (Forster and Epstein, 1964).

DePugh has still been active in recent years in dealing in heavy weaponry. He was arrested in September 1991 after authorities found nude photos of young girls and several weapons. He was convicted and later sentenced to 2 1/2 years in prison for possession of weapons by a convicted felon, possessing a mortar, an unregistered machine gun, and anti-aircraft missiles (Smith, 1991).

CHAPTER V

The Klans

Abraham Lincoln had been killed and with him died the promises he had made to reunite the South by honoring the former southern leaders and land holders and allowing them to have a decision making hand in healing the wounds of the Civil War. After succeeding him, Andrew Johnson was unable to carry on the idea of taking the good faith pledges of Confederate generals and statesmen that they would come back into the fold and try to reunify the nation. Congress took over Reconstruction and Republican radicals refused to treat the leaders of the conquered South as equals.

The northern army was sent in to be quartered in strategic cities. They were followed by scavengers. Former southern statesmen were barred from practicing law, voting, and even defending themselves in court. Unscrupulous southerners called "scalawags" and adventurers from the north with their belongings in carpet bags came to rape and pillage the South. Carpetbaggers recruited recently freed slaves, arming them and forming them into militia bands to support their coalition. When the Klan made its first rides, these newly freed blacks believed they were being attacked by ghosts because the Klansmen wore sheets and even covered their horses with white sheets (Cook, 1981).

The Ku Klux Klan originated in Pulaski, Tennessee, in 1865, when six young Confederate veterans gathered together in the wake of the Civil War. It was Christmas Eve of that year and their prospects were grim. They sought a diversion from their troubles and hard times and agreed to form a social club. Their sheets came from a desire to do some hazing, fraternity style, and they rode through the streets of town, dressed in sheets. When they discerned the chilling effect their nighttime excursions had on the freed blacks in the area, they began to get more serious and take more drastic actions (Turner, 1982). They had learned a way to still have some power in situations where they had previously been powerless and even ridiculed. The Klan had been born and continued recruiting as a secret organization that would give the South back some of its dignity in those difficult times.

The Klan grew in numbers and their violent activities increased. During the Klan's more than a century of existence, there have been at least five thousand documented lynchings of black people in the United States (Ginzburg, 1988).

From these humble beginnings rose the various Klans of today. The Klan went through several periods of upheaval and resurgence during the hundred years after the Reconstruction era to become the segmented organization it is today, but that detailed history is beyond the scope of this book. There are several books that detail this history. When emotional issues aggravate the public, the Klan comes forth as one hundred percent Americanism and fastens on causes, with deeply rooted prejudices, that whips up their followers into a frenzy (Cook, 1981).

Currently, the Klan is in a valley and many believe the Klan is dead, its more active members having become involved in other right wing organizations. However, the Klan's death knell has been sounded before and it has come back stronger. In recent years, the Klan has changed their image and it is such things as changing their image and their emphasis that has allowed them to survive and revive at various times in the past.

The targets of Klan attention have changed and the emphasis has changed, as the Klan went through periods of upheaval and resurgence. Their original targets were blacks and they branched out to include anyone they wished, from errant husbands to dishonest businessmen. When the Klan had a brief upsurge in 1915, they began to target Catholics and anyone they believed to be Catholic, Jewish, or a foreign immigrant, in addition to blacks. Immigrants with strange languages and religions had threatened the Klan's traditional values and became targets of the Klan (Loh, 1995).

When the Klan again grew in the 1960's during the civil rights disturbances, the Klan again targeted blacks, but began to exhibit increased anti-Semitic tendencies. The influx of northern civil rights workers, backed by the federal government, seemed like a replay of the Reconstruction era, and another degradation of the southern whites. The Klan revived and grew. The White Knights of Mississippi became the most vicious and violent to date, a ruthless band suspected of nearly three hundred terrorist acts, including the well known killing of three civil rights workers in Mississippi. Sam Holloway Bowers, Jr., led the White Knights at that time (Cook, 1981).

Since the first Klan began in the 1860's, the Klan has become three major separate affiliated organizations (see Appendix B), with several other unaffiliated chapters. The several Klans varied considerably in their purpose and procedure (Cook, 1962). Coming from their earlier days of black hatred, today's Klan is becoming more and more obsessed with the Jewish people, probably because of the influences of Christian Identity and the legacy of David Duke (ADL, 1991a).

The different Klans are distanced from each other, rarely cooperate, and have no central authorities. There is no KKK franchise, so it's just a matter of hooding up and ordering stationery with the blood-red KKK logo (Finch, 1983).

Numerous violent incidents in the 1980's brought publicity to the Klans, ranging from intimidation to cross burnings to burglary and murder. Klan groups adhere to the tenets of white supremacy with anti-Semitism as a central theme of their beliefs. Recently, the Klans have also tried to shed their violent image and indoctrinate youth and infiltrate the armed forces (ADL, 1988a). They have also tried to polish their public figures and become involved in the electoral process. The Klans also began associating with other right wing extremist groups, such as the Aryan Nations, Christian Identity groups, and other neo-Nazi groups (see Appendix C).

Jane Hardesty is the Director of the Cambridge, Massachusetts, Political Research Associates that study the right wing movement. In an AP story by Christopher Sullivan in 1990 (Sullivan, 1990), she indicated that white supremacists have devoted themselves to politics more seriously since the series of arrests in 1980's forced them to consider other mediums for their messages.

Klan members have gotten involved in the electoral process in a large way. J. B. Stoner ran for Lieutenant Governor in Georgia, Ralph Forbes for the same office in Arkansas and David Duke for the State Senate in Louisiana. Eva Sears of the Center for Democratic Renewal, an Atlanta-based organization that monitors the KKK and other groups, stated that "this is part of a new strategy that the white supremacists have developed. . . to work within the electoral system while at the same time building their underground operation" (Sullivan, 1990).

David Duke reported more than $600,000 in campaign donations. Forbes was a former American Nazi leader, and Stoner served a prison term for bombing a black church in Alabama in 1958. His avid black and anti-Semitic campaign put off some Democrat voters he had targeted (Sullivan, 1990).

UNITED KLANS OF AMERICA (UKA)

Robert Davidson and Calvin Craig, formerly of the Alabama Knights of the Ku Klux Klan, left the group because of infighting and formed the Invisible Empire, United Klans, Knights of the Ku Klux Klan of America, Inc. The name was later shortened to United Klans of America (UKA). Davidson resigned as Imperial Wizard in 1961 and in July 1961, the group united with Robert Shelton's Alabama Knights and Shelton became Grand Wizard of the UKA. Calvin Craig became Grand Dragon of the Georgia realm (George and Wilcox, 1992).

The United Klans of America (UKA) was probably the largest of the three national Klans in the 1960's and 1970's and probably still has more members, but they are an older and less active membership. Imperial Wizard Robert Shelton tried to keep the group, headquartered in Tuscaloosa, Alabama, as a clandestine order. There was little publicity until 1970 when twenty members were indicted in connection with violent racial incidents, and thirteen were convicted or pled guilty and served prison terms (ADL, 1988a; Suall and Lowe, 1987).

The UKA suffered another setback when it lost a $7 million settlement, including its national headquarters, to the family of a black youth hanged in 1981 by members of the UKA. Those who were charged attributed their inspiration to a cartoon of a black man being hanged, shown in *The Fiery Cross,* the official organ of the UKA. James Knowles, one of the two men convicted of the murder, testified that he and Henry Hays, now awaiting execution for the murder, killed the youth to show Klan strength in Alabama. The murder was allegedly ordered by Hays' father, Bennie Jack Hays, the UKA "Titan" or regional leader. Bennie Jack Hayes and Frank Cox, his son-in-law, were also indicted for the murder (ADL, 1988a).

Evidence that the UKA continued to participate in paramilitary training and terrorist activities came from the Florida Realm of the group in Pinellas County, Florida. Members of the Florida Realm were indicted for planning and training for terrorist acts against minorities, the first arrests under a law regarding paramilitary training in Florida (ADL, 1988a).

The UKA became largely defunct after suffering massive financial losses, losses of their national headquarters, and having their major leaders arrested. Former UKA members meet without national guidance and wait for Robert Shelton to reorganize or for a more traditional Klan to form that is more to their liking than the other national Klans (ADL, 1991a).

KNIGHTS OF THE KU KLUX KLAN

The 1970's saw increased rivalry and dissension among the Klans. David Duke incorporated his Knights of the Ku Klux Klan in Louisiana in 1974. He had briefly been active in the National Socialist White People's Party, and his career was plagued thereafter by a photo of him in a Nazi uniform (George and Wilcox, 1992).

The Knights of the Ku Klux Klan is made up of two separate factions. David Duke led one group in the 1970's, but quit in 1980, and turned over the crown to Alabama Grand Dragon, Don Black. Duke later lost his California organization which chose to become independent as the California Knights of the KKK with Tom Metzger as leader (see Appendix D).

Metzger later headed the White Aryan Resistance (WAR), which has little of the Klan ritual, has a "white rights stance" and National Socialist leanings. Duke went on to organize and lead an organization called the National Association for the Advancement of White People (NAAWP), which met with little success.

Don Black has a neo-Nazi background. He moved the Knights of the KKK to Tuscumbia, Alabama, and the first national conference, in 1980, was attended by Edward L. Fields, National Secretary of the National States' Rights Party. Fields claimed to have organized a substantial Klan movement in northern Georgia and implied it was part of the Knights of the KKK. Fields later called his new Klan the "New Order, Knights of the KKK." His appearance in the Klan movement was significant because he and his co-leader, J. B. Stoner, are among the most extreme, anti-Black, anti-Semitic hatemongers in the United States. Black has attempted to unite with other Klans. The newsletter of the group was called *The Crusader* but is now called *The White Patriot*, when it is published (ADL, 1988a).

Stanley McCollum of Tuscumbia, Alabama, leads the other and larger faction of the Knights of the KKK. He has strong ties to "Identity" leaders through his association with Thomas Robb, "Chaplain" of the KKK, who edits this Knights of the KKK paper, also called *The White Patriot* (ADL, 1988a). Thom Robb seeks to improve the Klan's image, using his authority as Grand Wizard to direct Klan units to make over their public image and participate in civic projects. Robb is also a pastor in the Identity-oriented Church of Jesus Christ-Christian, led by Richard Butler (ADL, 1991b).

McCollum spoke at a May 1987 rally at Identity minister Robert Miles' farm, vowing to fight federal sedition charges against Miles, Richard Butler of the Aryan Nations, and others. McCollum also participated in the 1987 Aryan Nations World Congress (ADL, 1988a).

NORTHWEST KNIGHTS OF THE KKK

Kim Badynski led one of the most visible and active factions of the Tuscumbia-based Knights, and this was outside the south, being headquartered in Chicago. Badynski has relocated to

Washington state with a group called the Northwest Knights of the KKK as part of the migration of white right wing extremists to that area to establish a white American homeland. Badynski has also been involved in Aryan Nations activities (ADL, 1988a; Suall and Lowe, 1987).

KNIGHTS OF THE KKK CONTINUE TO RECRUIT

The Knights of the KKK continue to hold public meetings to express their views and recruit new members. The Knights of the KKK held a rally outside the Franklin County Courthouse in Benton, Illinois, on April 8, 1995 (see photo section). Franklin County is a southern Illinois county whose local reputation has previously been that there were no blacks living in the county. This rally was billed as a "white Christian revival." Dennis McGiffen, Grand Dragon of the Illinois Knights of the KKK, labeled protestors at the rally as "AIDS infected lesbians and slimy queers." Troy Murphy, the Indiana KKKK Grand Dragon was also present (Lamczik, 1995).

An estimated five to eight hundred attended, with people coming and going during the rally. Many who attended were police officers and curiosity seekers. Some were protestors. Three Illinois state troopers with trained canines and several other troopers in riot gear were present in case of crowd disturbances. Officers on rooftops, in a helicopter, and sifting through the crowd completed their surveying of the situation (Pearson, "Tension. . .," 1995). Those who appeared in support of the Klan were often young, tattooed, and several had criminal records.

The purpose of the rally was to recruit new members for the Knights of the KKK. While such rallies attract attention and rally some support, the KKK of today is not the organized menace and lacks the sophisticated and widespread appeal of other growing right wing groups.

The greatest impact of the Klan rally in Benton, Illinois, appears to have been on the already strained resources of the Franklin County Sheriff's Department. They spent unbudgeted overtime to cover the event, and this was in addition to the reassignment of the Illinois State Police troopers who were present in great numbers (Pearson, KKK. . .," 1995).

This public rally in Illinois has been paralleled elsewhere in the country. In January 1993, a similar rally was held in Austin, Texas. It was attended by Michael Lowe of Waco, Texas, the Lone Star leader of the Knights of the KKK. Stanley McCollum, former Klan Grand Wizard, and Thom Robb, national KKKK leader, were also in attendance (*Southern Illinoisan*, 1993).

INVISIBLE EMPIRE, KNIGHTS OF THE KU KLUX KLAN

Bill Wilkinson began and led another of the largest Klan factions, the Invisible Empire, Knights of the Ku Klux Klan, from 1975-82. He had previously been David Duke's lieutenant, but broke with Duke to form his own group and was continually bickering and sniping with Duke, with Wilkinson the more aggressive of the two (George and Wilcox, 1992). The official organ of the group is *The Klansman*. Wilkinson sought a tough militant image and encouraged confrontation and open carrying of weapons (ADL, 1988a).

Wilkinson also tried for the leadership of a loosely-knit Klan organization with several thousand members, called the "Confederation of Independent Orders of the Invisible Empire, Knights of the KKK." The Confederate leaders saw him as being overly ambitious and chose Don Black from their own ranks as Imperial Wizard (ADL, 1988a).

Although periodic incidents of violence occurred, episodes became more frequent, and the level of violence increased as the decade of the 1980's approached. In 1979, Roger Handley, Wilkinson's Grand Dragon, and several others were involved in a bloody confrontation involving the conviction of a retarded black man for raping a white woman (ADL, 1988a).

By 1980, a major shift was seen in the Klan's role and they appeared to be trying to regain rather than protect their traditional white dominance in America (Chalmers, 1981). The Klan also began to be less of a clandestine organization. They held public rallies to show they were back in business and flourishing and not hiding behind hoods as in prior years (Shipp, 1981).

In July 1983, Wilkinson's Klansmen firebombed the offices of Klanwatch at the Southern Poverty Law Center. In May 1984,

Handley and other Klan leaders were charged with federal civil rights violations.

Nineteen eighty-five was an evolutionary year for the Klan. Changes were made in the structure and dealings of the Klan as they began an association (see Appendix C) with the Church of Jesus Christ-Christian, the Identity movement, and the Aryan Nations (Wade, 1987).

In 1982, Bill Wilkinson had allegedly provided information to the FBI, and his status as an FBI informant made him lose popular support and caused damage to the Klan. Then, in 1985, further damage was done when Wilkinson's ties to Soviet spy, John A. Walker, Jr., were revealed. Walker was the chief Klan organizer in the Norfolk, Virginia, area during the time he was providing U. S. Navy secrets to the Soviets (ADL, 1988a).

Wilkinson's immediate successor as Imperial Wizard was James Blair of Alabama, but his ill health forced his quick resignation. James W. Farrands of Shelton, Connecticut, a Roman Catholic, became Imperial Wizard of the Invisible Empire in 1986 and moved the group to Connecticut, making it the only national Klan outside the South (Suall and Lowe, 1987). In 1990, Farrands moved the group south again, to North Carolina, and promised to jump into electoral politics (Ridgeway, 1990).

LOUIS BEAM, KLAN POWERHOUSE

Louis Ray Beam, born August 20, 1946, has a long and illustrious history with Klan involvement and then with involvement with the Aryan Nations. He deserves separate mention because of the influence he has wielded and the changes he has brought to the Klan and other right wing extremist groups. Beam was first involved with Shelton's UKA, but then switched in 1976 to join David Duke's Knights of the Ku Klux Klan and became Texas Grand Titan of that group. He was actively involved in recruiting military personnel. In the late 1970's, he was promoted to Grand Dragon of the Texas Ku Klux Klan and became a member of the paramilitary arm of the KKK in Texas called the Texas Emergency Reserve (ADL, 1988a).

Beam was active in bigotry and violence against Vietnamese refugee shrimpers, with cross burnings and harassment. The

Vietnamese Fisherman's Association filed suit in federal court to prohibit the Klan from operating paramilitary training camps in Texas and won their suit. Beam resigned as Texas Grand Dragon of the Knights of the Ku Klux Klan in 1981. He later became Richard Butler's heir apparent and became Ambassador-at-Large for the Aryan Nations. He established the Aryan Nations computer network, the "Aryan Nations Liberty Net." He was a primary speaker at the 1983 Aryan Nations World Congress. Louis Beam was one of several charged by a federal grand jury with seditious conspiracy involving the Order and was a fugitive on the FBI's "Ten Most Wanted" list. After being apprehended in Mexico, he was found not guilty (ADL, 1988a). It was also Louis Beam who set up an assassination "point system" calling for the murder of police officers, federal officers and civil rights leaders (CDR, 1988).

UNAFFILIATED KLANS
Glenn Miller and the White Patriot Party

Glenn Miller of Angier, North Carolina, who began his extremist career as a neo-Nazi stormtrooper commander in the National Socialist Party of America, led a small Klan faction called the White Patriot Party. He stated that one thousand men would answer his trumpet call at Angier, dressed not in sheets, but combat fatigues, ready for race war (Flynn and Gerhardt, 1989, p. 10). According to grand jury testimony, a goodly amount of weaponry stolen from Fort Bragg and a nearby armory went to Miller and the White Patriot Party (Martinez and Guinther, 1988).

Glenn Miller was convicted in 1986 of engaging in illegal paramilitary training, and went underground in violation of his probation. He issued a declaration of war encouraging his followers to commit violent acts against federal officials and minorities. This "declaration of war" was similar to that seen with Bob Mathews and the Order.

Federal agents arrested Miller and three heavily armed compatriots in the Missouri Ozarks, and Miller pled guilty to charges of mailing the "Declaration of War" and possessing hand grenades. Miller entered the federal witness' protection program in September 1987 after testifying against other right wing extremists before a Fort Smith grand jury. The White Patriot Party regrouped itself under Cecil Cox, after Millers' conviction, calling itself the Southern National Front. In 1987, they announced plans to merge with the National Democratic Front, led by Gary Gallo (ADL, 1988a).

NATIONAL STATES' RIGHTS PARTY

Edward Fields and Jesse B. Stoner formed the National States' Rights Party in 1958. Stoner was a lawyer, KKK organizer, and called Adolf Hitler a moderate. Both men were associated with anti-Jewish sentiments. The National States's Rights Party had managed to absorb several other right wing groups, such as the Conservative Party, National White American Party, and the North Carolina Knights of the Ku Klux Klan (George and Wilcox, 1992). The National States' Rights Party has been an anti-black, anti-Jewish hybrid organization of neo-Nazi and Klan groups (ADL, 1988a)

Stoner ran for office many times. He was indicted and served prison time. Fields has been the primary figure in the NSRP as National Secretary and editor of *The Thunderbolt*. He formed a Ku Klux Klan group in Georgia called the New Order Knights of the KKK in the late 1970's but it was of short duration (George and Wilcox, 1992).

Fields and Stoner have targeted both Jews and blacks. Fields travels abroad to speak on related topics. Matt Koehl of the New Order was once involved with the NSRP, as was James K. Warner, although Koehl's present group, the New Order, is not the same as the New Order Knights. Warner then moved on to form the Sons of Liberty and Christian Defense League. The NSRP disbanded in turmoil in 1984 after more than twenty-five years. Stoner was away in jail and Fields could not cope with the organization alone. He won rights to continue publishing *The Thunderbolt* and changed its name in 1988 to *The Truth at Last*. Stoner got out of jail in 1986 and founded His Crusade Against Corruption, a one-man operation, praising the AIDS virus, calling it a racial disease (George and Wilcox, 1992).

NATIONAL KNIGHTS OF THE KU KLUX XLAN

The National Knights of the Ku Klux Klan, led by James Venable of Decatur, Georgia, was once a strong challenger to the United Klans of America. The National KKKK had closer connections to the original Klan of the 19th century. Wilkinson then recruited the militants from the National Knights to join the UKA and the group became mostly trappings and ceremony and little action (Finch, 1983).

OTHER SMALLER KLANS

There are also numerous other small Klan factions which are unaffiliated in many cases. None of the other Klans are national in scope, but the one that comes closest is Virgil Griffin's Christian Knights of the Ku Klux Klan, in Holly, North Carolina. Griffin is known for his participation in a 1969 incident in Greensboro, North Carolina, in which five Communist Workers' Party members died in a street battle with Klansmen and neo-Nazis. The Christian Knights exist in about half a dozen states and their favorite tactic is street marches to gain publicity and attract new members (ADL, 1991a).

The Knights of the White Camellia of the Ku Klux Klan in Texas have tried to garner more attention, with some success. Grand Dragon Charles Lee headquarters his group in the Pasadena area. The Texas Klan has been down to its lowest level in several years, partly due to Louis Beam's arrest for sedition, and his ensuing flight from justice, although he was later acquitted of the charge.

Bill Albers of Modesto, California, leads an independent group called American Knights of the KKK. He is closely linked to the Aryan Nations (ADL, 1988a).

Another interesting development in 1987 was a court order forcing Alex Young, a former Jefferson County, Kentucky, police officer to reveal names of the Confederate Officers Patriot Squad (COPS). This is a faction whose members are reportedly most police officers (ADL, 1988a).

There are several other small Klan groups in many states, most of them not too noteworthy. The Southern White Knights of Georgia split with James Venable's National Knights of the KKK because they were not militant enough. The splits and factionalisms are common with the small Klans and fights for leadership.

Robert Miles also promoted what he called the "Fifth Era Klan" which would be a new Klan emphasizing anti-Semitism and neo-Nazism in all countries that are traditionally white lands in modern times. His strategy called for returning to the original status as a secret organization of hard core militants devoted to preserving white supremacy. There are many other Klan groups that have made small gains in various parts of the country. The White Knights exist in Florida, and Independent Order Knights and Conference of Independent Knights are in Maryland. The New Order Knights are in Missouri and the Invisible Empire Knights are in New Jersey. The White Unity Party of Pennsylvania and Ohio Knights are also Klan factions. The White Knights of the KKK in New York and Forsyth County Defense League in Georgia continue the list, which goes on and on. There is no point in naming all the small factions nationwide. There are many of them and only the major players have been dealt with in the preceding pages.

The Klan's decade long decline has slowed and it continues to recruit new members, although as an organization, the Klan is not seen as having major strengths at this point in history. It is, however, no longer experiencing the steady loss of strength it suffered in the 1980's. Major KKK leaders urge their followers to abandon overtly violent tactics, and put forth a more positive image, dealing with current issues, to recruit new members. This urge to avoid violence has been the result of such actions as Tom Metzger and the White Aryan Resistance (WAR) being held accountable civilly for inciting skinheads to commit criminal acts, including murder.

This revisionist policy is for tactical reasons and not because such people as James Farrands and Thom Robb have had a change of heart. Looking at the Klan leaders mentioned, such people as Wilkinson, Duke, Metzger, Glenn Miller, and Thom Robb, it is clear that they are lifelong supremacists who have found their calling as "career extremists," gathering their forces for the cause.

CHAPTER VI

Neo-Nazi Groups

Neo-Nazi groups associated with Hitler-like activities existed even prior to Hitler's demise (Strong, 1941). These included the Silver Shirts of the 1930's. Henry Beach, who cofathered the Posse Comitatus, was a member of this group. The neo-Nazi movement in America is characterized by small numbers and large capacity to generate media coverage. The term has often been overused and as a synonym for anti-Semite and racist, but not all anti-Semitic and racist groups use Nazi symbolism (George and Wilcox, 1992), nor wish the identification with neo-Nazis. It will be used here to mean generally those who use traditional Nazi symbolism, self-identify with Nazi ideas, or show respect or reverence for Adolf Hitler and the Third Reich.

GERALD L. K. SMITH AND WESLEY SWIFT

The Silver Shirts were founded by William Dudley Pelley, who wanted to be the American Hitler and ran for President on the Christian Party ticket in 1936. Gerald L. K. Smith founded the Christian Nationalist Church, which supported Mussolini and Hitler. He was one of the first to join the Silver Shirts. Smith was an important figure for the far right, the link between the 30's fascism and the white resistance of today.

Wesley Swift, also of the Ku Klux Klan, was Smith's right-hand man. Swift made radio broadcasts advocating destroying all Jews. After Smith's death, Swift became acquainted with William Potter Gale, and through him, Richard Butler, then an aircraft parts manufacturer (Ridgeway, 1990). Butler helped Swift organize the Christian Defense League in the 1960's, which Butler inherited upon Rev. Swift's death in 1971. Butler tried to join Gale's Posse and another group, the Emancipation of the White Seed, but each group's leader wanted to be the boss, and that merge failed (Vaughn, 1985).

Following World War II, neo-Nazi groups came into public view with an active membership, although they were not generally associated with right wing activities. The American Nazi Party in the 1950's was the first to be well organized and nationally recognized. There are several organized neo-Nazi groups, several loosely organized groups such as skinhead factions, and connections with other extremist groups, such as Christian Identity and Klan groups (see Appendix E). These small scattered groups reflect the fractured nature of the movement, although organization seems to be improving.

AMERICAN NAZI PARTY

George Lincoln Rockwell founded the American Nazi Party in 1958, later known as the National Socialist White People's Party and currently known as the New Order. This group was never large in numbers, with more people subscribing to *The Storm-trooper* and *The Rockwell Report* than were actually members. This group pledged its allegiance to Nazi Germany and the late Adolf Hitler. This was in contrast to the KKK, which had its roots in native America.

Rockwell was assassinated in August 1967 by a party dissident, John Patler. There was much dissension in the party and it was taken over by Matthias (Matt) Koehl, who had been one of the founders of the National States Rights Party in 1958. Koehl depended heavily upon two national officers, Robert Lloyd and William Pierce (George and Wilcox, 1992).

In 1968, the party, renamed the National Socialist White People's Party, moved to Arlington, Virginia, and continued to be directed at youth with a goal of a Nazi-style regime in this country. Several splinter groups formed in the 1970's, including the National White People's Party, led by Charles White of Asheville, North Carolina; the White Party of America in Washington, D.C., led by Karl Allen, and an American Nazi Party, led by John Robert Bishop, and headquartered in Davenport, Iowa (ADL, 1988a).

The neo-Nazi movement has steadily declined, but a number of these small groups have survived. The oldest and most stable is still the New Order, previously called the National Socialist White People's Party, which has been led for more than twenty years by Matt Koehl. It is better organized, disciplined, and experienced, tactically more cautious, and more inflexible to the fidelity to the original Nazi principles than its competitors. It emphasizes white racism as much as anti-Semitism. The New Order has relocated to New Berlin, Wisconsin, and seeks to form a "National Socialist community called 'Nordland'" (ADL, 1988).

WILLIAM PIERCE AND THE NATIONAL ALLIANCE

William Pierce split with Matt Koehl and the National Socialist White People's Party (now New Order) in 1970 (George and Wilcox, 1992). William Pierce is a former physics professor from Oregon State University. He began the current National Alliance in 1974 (*Dominion Post*, 4/14/91). The organization was formerly headquartered in Washington, D.C. This group and the Cosmotheist Church, the religious wing of the group, moved to Mill Point, West Virginia in 1985. The Cosmotheist Church was based on natural law and self-realization, rather than spiritual law (The Cosmotheist Church). The church building may now be used for other purposes, as the group has expanded enterprises in printing and radio programs.

The National Alliance was formerly known as the National Youth Alliance and under the control of Willis Carto of the Liberty Lobby, but broke with him in 1970. The publication of the group is the *National Vanguard*, formerly called *Attack!* There has also been an internal organ called *National Alliance Bulletin*, formerly called *Action* (ADL, 1988). The National Alliance is second only to the Aryan Nations in prominence and influence within the white supremacy movement today (Searls, 1995).

The National Alliance has also had many ties to the Aryan Nations, with Robert Mathews of the National Alliance combining with Aryan Nations and Klan members to form the Order and with William Pierce recently renewing his ties by attending the Aryan Nations World Congress in 1995.

Pierce is also a principal in "American Dissident Voices," a radio program broadcast on AM radio stations and shortwave across the country (Lambrecht, 1995). Transcripts of his radio broadcasts are available through National Vanguard Books, the publishing enterprise associated with William Pierce.

A flyer encouraging listeners to tune into "American Dissident Voices" is entitled "Free Money." It lists its view of how to get free money in America: be an 80-IQ welfare mom having illegitimate children every nine months; be a homosexual "performance artist"; a foreign dictator in the good graces of New World Order elitists; someone who burns their own neighborhood, etc. The flyer states that this "free money" is not available to working white Americans because their job is to provide this "free money." This flyer encourages people who are interested in restoring America to her rightful owners to listen to the radio broadcasts every week (National Alliance, undated).

William Pierce published *The Turner Diaries*, an account chronicling the violent takeover of the United States by racial extremists trying to rid the country of non-Aryans. In the book, violent revolution followed the fictional Cohen Act, which outlawed private ownership of guns (Macdonald, 1980). Earl Turner, the subject of the book, is a member of the Organization, a right wing group that starts a race war against the System, including extreme violence to eliminate Jews, blacks, and passive whites *(Dominion Post, 1991)*. Pierce used the pseudonym Andrew McDonald. *The Turner Diaries* was allegedly used as a handbook by Robert Mathews of the Order, for whom Pierce was mentor.

It was shortly after an alleged transfer of funds from the Order in 1984 that Pierce acquired a 346-acre compound in West Virginia. Pierce paid for the real estate with $95,000 cash, according to Jerry Dale, former Pocahontas County Sheriff, who is the area's self appointed watchdog to Pierce and the one who located Pierce in their area in 1986 (Dale, 7/6/95).

The Cosmotheist Church gained tax exempt status in 1978, although tax exempt status was denied the National Alliance that same year, both being headquartered in Mill Point, West Virginia, in Pocahontas County. Many essentially political and partisan groups incorporate in this manner for tax exempt status (Forster and Epstein, 1964). After protests from the ADL, the tax exempt status was revoked by the IRS, and this revocation was upheld by a federal appeals court in 1983 on the basis of the church's white supremacist beliefs (George and Wilcox, 1992).

Pierce indicated that his church would concern itself with the fitness of our race for survival. He indicated that he had the intention of training his warriors for that cause (ADL, 1987a).

An NBC "Dateline" broadcast on April 25, 1995, pointed out that the bombing of the Federal Building in Oklahoma City was also "blueprinted" in *The Turner Diaries*. William Pierce was interviewed on this broadcast and stated he was not responsible for how his book was used. Morris Dees of the Southern Poverty Law Center had pointed out coincidences in the book and the bombing incident and caused a flood of media from all over the country, and even outside the country, to travel to the isolated and tiny community of Mill Point, West Virginia (Pritt, 5/4/95).

There is also a sequel to *The Turner Diaries* called *Hunter*, (Macdonald, 1989) in which the hero is described by Delta Press as a former combat pilot in Vietnam "who surveys the race mixing, the open homosexuality... finds that for him there is really no choice at all: he is compelled to fight the evil which afflicts America in the 1990's." The description continues, "In *The Turner Diaries*, author Andrew Macdonald showed the outcome of what is going on in society right now. Now, in *Hunter*, he shows what one man does to combat it before it gets that far" (Delta Press, 1995). At this point, no one has claimed that *Hunter* has been used as a pattern for criminal activities. However, the 1993 conspiracy to start a race war by bombing a well known black Los Angeles church is very similar to actions and sentiments described in *Hunter*.

Bill Lambrecht discussed the similarities in the Oklahoma City bombing and the fictional account in *The Turner Diaries* in the *Post Dispatch* of St. Louis, Missouri on April 26, 1995, after the bombing (Lambrecht, 1995). In the novel, a bomb made of ammonium nitrate fertilizer is packed into a delivery truck and detonated at 9:15 a.m. beneath the FBI headquarters in Washington, D.C., killing hundreds.

The actual event in Oklahoma City was quite similar, down to the type of bomb and the time of day it detonated. William Pierce was interviewed in this news article and stated that he had checked his data base and none of the suspects was a member of his National Alliance. He stated, ". . .the unfortunate fact is that violence breeds violence. And when you have a government that engages in terrorist activity against its citizens, you have to accept that citizens will strike back against the government." Pierce argued that the federal government brought the bombing on itself by storming the Branch Davidian compound in Waco two years ago. Pierce stated, "Something new is about to happen, I believe. A growing number of Americans have such a hatred of the government in Washington that some of them will commit desperate and foolish acts like the Oklahoma City bombing. A growing number will turn to terrorism as their only weapon against a terrorist government" (Lambrecht, 1995, 5b).

Pam Pritt is a writer for *The Pocahontas Times*, a weekly paper located in Marlinton, West Virginia, county seat of the county where Pierce resides. Pierce denied to her that he was the inspiration or had any prior knowledge of the Oklahoma City bombing. He said, "Our task is to develop media for reaching people with ideas. Any attack on the government would hinder our cause. It is not a productive way to go. We can't challenge the federal government at this point. We leave them alone and hope they leave us alone" (Pritt, 4/27/95, p. 2).

Pierce discounts the media attention about such things as the Oklahoma City bombing and the National Alliance member arrested for possessing a bubonic plague virus. He told Pam Pritt (5/18/95, p. 2) in reference to all the recent media attention, "I think it's gotten to the point that when anyone does something that seems extremist, the media comes running to Hillsboro [another small town nearby and where the post office Pierce's group uses for a mailing address is located]. The media goes to quasi-official sources instead of doing its own research to find out about someone who's not mainstream, if he's white and non-Jewish." Pierce said that he had been in the area for ten years and just writes there, that the people of Pocahontas County had nothing to fear from him.

Shotgun News in April 1990 had an advertisement for an "airtight burial vault" in which guns and ammunition could be buried. The address given for "Vanguard Security Systems" was the same as National Vanguard Books (Dale, 1995; *Shotgun News*, 1990). This just gives an idea as to the various enterprises operated from the small compound on the West Virginia mountainside.

William Pierce is a former associate professor of physics at Oregon State University. He was a graduate student of the California Institute of Technology and once worked at the Jet Propulsion Laboratory in Pasadena, California (*Post Dispatch*, 4/24/95).

William Pierce's National Alliance sits on a large plot of isolated, wooded, West Virginia mountainside (see photo section). The entrances are padlocked and lead up the side of a steep mountain. Mill Point does not have a Post Office and is just a wide spot in the road with a lumber mill and a bait and tackle shop whose owner often gets asked how to find Dr. Pierce. Mill Point is located on Route 55 west of Marlinton, and east of Richwood. The compound, seen from an aerial view, consists of a very large pole-barn-type structure with the National Alliance symbol. This was built for the Cosmotheist Church. Dr. Pierce's mobile home and a few other small structures dot the hillside (Dale, 7/6/95). Pocahontas County is located in an area known for limestone caves and underground rivers, both probably useful for groups into survivalism.

Dr. Pierce has authored many monographs, some of which are the basis for his radio programs. In "The Roots of Civilization," he discusses his ideas of black inferiority in that blacks not only score lower on standard IQ tests, but also have an inability to reason inferentially. He attributes the paucity of blacks in professions requiring abstract reasoning to this inherent problem. Dr. Pierce believes that this ability to reason, to exhibit "Yankee ingenuity" is a racial trait (Pierce, "The Roots of Civilization, 1994).

William Pierce has also spoken extensively on gun control. In a speech given over "American Dissident Voices" radio program on January 29, 1994, he stated that most of those who choose to give up their weapons when called to do so by the government do so because they trust the government.

Pierce stated his belief that the changes in attitude in the American public stem from several reasons, including the change from rural to urban. People in rural areas were always more self-sufficient because they had to be, not having the services of city protection.

He also points out his belief that since women began voting in 1920, they shifted the burden of personal protection from the individual to the government because women do not have basic, instinctive self-defense ideas. Finally, he points to a stream of immigrants in latter years that came here to receive welfare checks and promoted an underclass of citizens dependent upon the government.

Pierce points to a fourth factor that he says dwarfs the others, the growing influence that Jews have had on public opinion by their control of the mass media information and entertainment. Pierce says that America's problem is not guns, but race, that crime and violence in America is a direct and immediate consequence of the loss of racial homogeneity in American society (Pierce, "Gun Control Not What It Seems," 1994).

While Pierce's views are abhorrent to most, he expresses them well. Over the years, he has authored a great deal of material, used his radio messages, and made contact over computers with many who do agree with his views.

Experts view Pierce as one of the most influential figures over the years in the white supremacist movement. Mira Boland, who is research director for the Anti-Defamation League, believes that Pierce's membership is in the thousands, but his influence far exceeds that and he has gained respect over the years for his intellect and writing style. Laird Wilcox who has coauthored a book on political extremism, believes that Pierce has repelled allies by his style, which is contentious, idiosyncratic, paranoid, and hard to get along with, like the characters in his books (Lambrecht, 1995).

White supremacists met in late July 1995 at the Aryan Nations compound in Hayden Lake, Idaho, for the annual meeting of the Aryan Nations' World Congress. William Pierce agreed to speak at that meeting, the first time he has made an approach to other neo-Nazi organizations in years. There is speculation that he was making a move to fill the leadership vacuum in the national neo-Nazi, white supremacy movement, which has been mostly splintered for the past quarter of a century. Pierce makes no secret of his message of racism and believes that breakdowns in family relationships and a rise in crime can all be attributed to a breakdown in racial purity (Searls, 1995). Perhaps after July 1995, Dr. Pierce will be spreading his message to an even bigger audience.

TOM METZGER AND
THE WHITE ARYAN RESISTANCE (WAR)

Tom Metzger, formerly of the California Knights of the Ku Klux Klan, founded the White Aryan Resistance (WAR). WAR was formerly called the White American Political Association (WAPA). He is one of the best known white supremacists in America. He started a cable television series, "Race and Reason" and was the reported recipient of one quarter of a million dollars from the Order's robberies. Metzger also appears on national television talk shows, in the company of skinheads and other right wing extremists (ADL, 1989). The group's publication is also called *WAR* (George and Wilcox, 1992).

The White Aryan Resistance is technologically advanced, using computer bulletin boards, video tapes, and taped phone messages at various locations around the country (George and Wilcox, 1992). In 1984, WAR joined other white supremacist groups in operating a computerized bulletin board to deliver hate messages and provide announcements of upcoming Klan and neo-Nazi meetings and contact with other "patriotic" organizations (ADL, 1988a).

Metzger also initiated the White Student Union (WSU), also called the Aryan Youth Movement, or AYM, to encourage student participation. There were twenty WSU chapters operating in 1986 (Martinez and Guinther, 1988). The White

Student Union was operated by Greg Withrow until he became disenchanted with the cause, and his previous followers nailed his hands, crucifixion-style, to a plank. This type of violent and aberrant behavior is condoned by such radical right wing groups for those considered traitors. Metzger's son, John, was then appointed WSU President (ADL, 1988a). Tom Metzger has also promoted the growth of the skinhead movement more than any other right wing leader (George and Wilcox, 1992).

The White Aryan Resistance, in a recorded telephone message, advocates that abortion is part of a Jewish plot to take over the world. This is in close adherence to the doctrine of the Posse Comitatus (Hoffman, 1986).

NATIONAL SOCIALIST LIBERATION FRONT
The National Socialist Liberation Front, originating in California in the early 1970's and now of Louisiana, has been the most violent of the Nazi splinter groups. Its founder, Joseph Tomassi, former west coast leader of the American Nazi Party, was killed in 1975 by a National Socialist White People's Party member. Donald C. Rust headed the NSLF until he went to prison on a federal firearms charge. The NSLF claimed credit for bombing the office of the Socialist Worker's Party in February 1975 and engaged in violence against the National Socialist White People's Party.

Karl Hand, former KKK member and Grand Dragon for David Duke, associated with the National Socialist Liberation Front in 1981 and ran it with his wife, Mary Sue, until 1986 when he went to prison in Louisiana for a fifteen-year term for attempted murder. Mary Sue married Hand in a 1985 ceremony over which Robert Miles of the Mountain Church officiated. She calls herself the "First Lady of the Sword" (Suall and Lowe, 1987). After Hand's incarceration, he encouraged his followers to join Tom Metzger and the White Aryan Resistance (ADL, 1989).

OTHER NEO-NAZI GROUPS
Socialist National Aryan People's Party
Keith Gilbert was first recruited by Richard Butler and the Aryan Nations. He went on to found the Socialist National

Aryan People's Party of Post Falls, Idaho until he went to prison on welfare fraud charges in 1985. He previously served time for planning to explode several pounds of dynamite in an attempt to kill Martin Luther King, Jr.

NATIONAL SOCIALIST VANGUARD

The National Socialist Vanguard, formerly of Salinas, California, moved to the Dallas, Oregon, and Goldendale, Washington, areas. Its principals are Dan Stewart, formerly of the National Socialist White People's Party, Fred Turner, and Rick Cooper. This group expressed a desire to build a neo-Nazi community called "Wolf Stadt." They praised the Order and its activities in their publication, *The NSV Report* (ADL, 1988a). This group likely is composed primarily of its leaders with no real membership (George and Wilcox, 1992).

SOUTHERN NATIONAL FRONT

The Southern National Front, already discussed with the Klan, is really a hybrid of the Klan and a neo-Nazi organization. It was formerly Glenn Miller's White Patriot Party. There was evidence that this group received $50,000 of the cash stolen by the Order (Suall and Lowe, 1987). Glenn Miller also aped Robert Mathews' "Declaration of War" and adopted Louis Beam's point system for Aryan Warriors (Martinez and Guinther, 1988).

LIBERTY LOBBY

Willis Carto heads the Liberty Lobby, the most professional and successful anti-Jewish propaganda organization in the United States (ADL, 1985c). Willis Carto was a California businessman when he published *Right* from 1955-60, a monthly newsletter compiling materials from right wing sources, with an emphasis on anti-Communism and conspiracy theories. Liberty Lobby, his primary operation, was founded in 1957 and at the end of the 1960's, the monthly *Liberty Letter* had a circulation of more than 200,000. *Liberty Lowdown, Western Destiny, and Washington Observer* appeared later. In 1966, Carto bought *American Mercury Magazine* and quit publishing *Western Destiny*. The *Mercury* had long had a staff of extreme right writers, including John Birch

Society supporters, Gerald L. K. Smith, and Minutemen members (George and Wilcox, 1992). The *Liberty Letter* ended in 1975, changing to the *National Spotlight*, which later shortened to *The Spotlight*. In 1980, *American Mercury* and *Washington Observer* stopped publication. Carto founded the National Youth Alliance in November 1968 with remnants of Youths for Wallace. Nazi symbolism was used at meetings. William Pierce also became involved with the National Youth Alliance. After legal battles with Carto because of conflicts over who was running the show, a dissident group broke away to become the National Alliance, led by William Pierce (George and Wilcox, 1992).

The Spotlight now has a circulation of one quarter of a million readers (Flynn and Gerhardt, 1989). Liberty Lobby also publishes *The Zionist Watch,* and founded the Populist Party as a vehicle to forward their aims. The Liberty Lobby, as well as other propaganda pushers, has promoted concerns of more militant right wing extremists and praised the leaders and martyrs of the cause (ADL, 1985c). The Populist Party is still putting forth candidates to further conservative and right wing positions. Bo Gritz, who mediated an end to the Randy Weaver standoff, has been a Populist Party candidate. Gritz has established a right wing community called "Almost Heaven" in Idaho.

GEORGE DIETZ

George Dietz, a farm broker and one time member of the Hitler Youth, migrated to the United States in 1957. He is a major publisher and supplier of neo-Nazi literature. He was also the first radical extremist to establish a computer bulletin board to be accessed through home computers for the "cause" (Suall and Lowe, 1987).

He has not been tied to violent acts. He has, however, helped distribute information that has assisted groups in recruitment and furthering their cause.

NATIONAL SOCIALIST PARTY OF AMERICA

Frank Collins was National Socialist White People's Party midwest coordinator until he was dismissed by Matt Koehl. He then formed the National Socialist Party of America (NSPA) in 1970 (George and Wilcox, 1992). He continued to lead the NSPA in the 1970's until he pled guilty in 1980 to indecent liberties with a number of teenage and preteenage boys and was sentenced to seven years in prison. The bimonthly tabloid of the group was called *The New Order* and its German counterpart was called *NS Kampfruf* (ADL, 1988).

Harold Covington assumed the leadership of the group in 1980. Helping Covington rise to this position was Collins' discovery of child pornography at the Nazi headquarters. It was this discovery for which Chicago's Youth Division arrested Collins, who had taken photos of himself and his male juvenile victims (George and Wilcox, 1992).

Covington made news when he filed in the Republican primary for attorney general of Illinois and won 43% of the vote, making national headlines. Covington had been leader of the North Carolina unit of the NSPA, when the infamous shootout took place between members of the Communist Workers Party and the KKK in Greensboro, North Carolina. Two of the Klansmen involved were also NSPA members. The subsequent trial and heavy media coverage made Covington the most recognizable neo-Nazi in the country (George and Wilcox, 1992).

In 1982, a new American Nazi Party was founded as a reconstituted branch of the NSPA. Jim Burford led this group. They publish *The Public Voice* and *ANP Newsletter* (ADL, 1988a).

NATIONAL SOCIALIST GERMAN WORKERS PARTY OVERSEAS ORGANIZATION

An American, Gary Rex Lauck, headed a group, begun in 1974, called the National Sozialistische Deutsche Arbeiter Partei-Auslands Organisation. This is German for the National Socialist German Workers Party - Overseas Organization. He has been active in smuggling neo-Nazi literature into West Germany and has lived in Chicago, where he formerly worked with the now defunct National Socialist Party of America, although the organization has a Nebraska mailing address.

Lauck says that Hitler's greatest shortcoming was that he was too humane. Lauck has become a latter-day Joseph Goebbels for the illegal neo-Nazi government in Germany. Government officials continually identified him as the leading source of banned Nazi propaganda and memorabilia. Because of increased neo-Nazi and rightist violence, during which raids Laucks' literature constantly turned up in possession of activists, the authorities stepped up their campaign to arrest Lauck. Lauck said if the FBI wanted to do anything about him, they would have to violate the First Amendment rights of a native-born citizen on behalf of a foreign government seeking to suppress freedom of speech (Worthington, 1994).

Lauck, of Lincoln, Nebraska, was arrested March 20, 1995, while visiting neo-Nazi friends in Copenhagen, Denmark and Denmark agreed to extradite him back to Germany. He was the main supplier of illegal fascist propaganda to Germany, according to the German Justice Ministry. Lauck operated from the United States because he was protected by free speech guarantees (Southern Illinoisan, 5/9/95). This group publishes *The New Order* in English and *NS Kampfruf* in German (George and Wilcox, 1992).

SECURITY SERVICE (SS) ACTION GROUP

John Morierty and Edward Dunn formed the Security Services (SS) Action Group in Dearborn, Michigan, after breaking with Casey Kalemba's United White People's Party in 1979. Their publications, *S.S. Action Group Michigan Briefing* and *Aryans Awake,* feature news stories about their clashes with counter-demonstrators. They have a small membership and few who show up at these demonstrations (George and Wilcox, 1992).

The group publishes periodicals that advocate wiping out Jews and handbills disparaging Jews, blacks, and other minority groups. They have attended gatherings with the American Nazi Party in Chicago to celebrate Hitler's birthday. Dunn has been charged in federal indictments for drug and weapons charges (ADL, 1988a).

CHAPTER VII

Cooperating Groups
Difficult to Classify

THE LAROUCHEANS

L yndon Hermyle LaRouche, Jr., was born of Quaker parents in 1922 and after serving as a medic/conscientious objector in the United States Army, he became involved in Communist party activities. He became involved with Students for a Democratic Society (SDS), a leftist group. LaRouche has been considered "left" and "right" because of the group's strange ideology. LaRouche's National Democratic Policy Committee's enemies are international bankers, the Federal Reserve System and Trilateralists, Nazis, Jesuits, Zionists, and the KKK, among others. He appears to cater to right wing groups when he wants their support (George and Wilcox, 1992).

LaRouche operated an international complex of corporations, political fronts, political committees, and cultural and scientific projects to further his beliefs and raise money for his purposes. He ran afoul of the law later in some of his fund raising endeavors (ADL, 1988a).

LaRouche ran for President in 1984 calling himself a conservative Democrat (the Democrats denied any connections with him) and forgetting his leftist and rightist leanings. LaRouche later became involved in credit card and loan fraud schemes and he and several followers were tried in federal court in Virginia in 1988, convicted on several counts and went to federal prison (George and Wilcox, 1992). Several LaRouche candidates on state slates have been nominated because they had names similar to "real" Democrat candidates or simply because none of the candidates were well known and the LaRouche candidates had names as American as apple pie.

What was particularly disturbing to mainstream American Democrats was that candidates who so clearly did not represent the views of those voting could be nominated for important political offices. Since the first disastrous elections in which LaRouche candidates prevailed, the Democrat party has made efforts to publicize who their candidates are **and** who their candidates are not.

JEWS FOR THE PRESERVATION
OF FIREARMS OWNERSHIP (JPFO)

Political causes such as gun control make strange bedfellows. For the most part, right wing groups disparage Jews and attribute their problems to Jewish control of the media and a desire for one world government. However, literature distributed at militia meetings contains several pieces of information from the Jews for the Preservation of Firearms Ownership (JPFO), this along with information from more right wing and anti-Semitic groups. JPFO information, for instance, was passed out side by side with *Operation Vampire Killer 2000*, which discusses conspiracy theories and Jewish control of the media.

JPFO, in their publications, discusses that they have unearthed original texts of numerous gun control laws in countries that subsequently practiced genocide. The laws were said to be passed by governments not intent on genocide, but rather that their successors had used the same laws to carry out mass extermina-tions of their political enemies.

Charlie Reese of the *Orlando Sentinel* (1993), discussed an interview with Aaron Zelman, executive director of Jews for the Preservation of Firearms Ownership. Zelman shows similarities in the Nazi Gun Control Act of 1938 and the U. S. Gun Control Act of 1968, and along with Jay Simkin, Research Director of JPFO, alleges proof that the late Senator Thomas Dodd of Connecticut had the Library of Congress translate the German original into English just before the passage of the 1968 Gun Control Act.

JPFO believes that the greatest killer of its citizenry has always been the government (especially of Jews) and that America was founded for its citizens to be free from fear and protected by the Constitutional right to own firearms. These firearms would be for personal defense and if necessary, against a tyrannical government (Reese, 1993).

Jay Simkin (March, 1994) makes a point that is sure to be popular with right wing gun control opponents. He says that the argument that criminals' abuse of firearms justifying gun control is disproved in that there is hard data to prove that criminals rarely abuse military-style rifles. He further points out that it is unclear why criminal activity should define the civil rights of the law abiding.

This author requested information from the organization and received a "fact sheet" entitled "Introduction" with a membership form on the back. This fact sheet states that the organization was founded in 1989, has 4,000 members in the United States and other countries, and has one goal, the destruction of the idea that "gun control" is a socially useful public policy in any country. The fact sheet goes on to state that this organization can show that Jewish Law (the Five Books of Moses and the Talmud) mandates self-defense. The fact sheet states that the organization is tax-exempt, educational and knows that genocide is the down-side to gun control. The organization is open to all law-abiding persons of all races. Their various publications point to genocide coming from gun control and include *The Firearms Sentinel* with membership (JPFO, 1995).

Jews for the Preservation of Firearms Ownership is in direct opposition to the Anti-Defamation League of B'nai B'rith. The ADL has always been the best known defender of the Jewish faith and rights and the JPFO alleges that they are wrong in their approach and are paving the way for the next genocide of the Jewish race.

CHAPTER VIII

Skinhead Groups

S kinhead groups began In this country about 1984 (ADL, 1988a; 1987d). The Anti-Defamation League of B'nai B'rith (ADL, 1990) first learned of them when Chicago Area Skinheads (CASH), also known as Romantic Violence, attended gatherings at Robert Miles' farm. They are generally younger than the other types of extremists, in the late teens to early twenties, with shaved or closely cropped hair, jeans, suspenders, and combat boots (Burden, 1992).

GANG ORGANIZATION

Skinhead groups have traits similar to other youth "gang" type organizations including the age group recruited, use of alcohol and illegal drugs, gang structure, tattooing, colors, name and common dress and criminal behavior (Coplon, 1988, p. 56). The danger from skinheads is that their activities are a way of life, not just the result of them joining an organization. The violence is intrinsic to their way of life. The skinheads provide an energizing influence to the entire hate movement. Skinhead violence inflicted on an already tense racial situation could cause massive violence in the form of riots (ADL, 1990).

VIOLENT THRILL SEEKERS

Skinheads typify the "thrill seeker" of the typology, regarding individuals who perpetrate violence against targeted minorities. They are young, very active, and very violent. While they commit criminal offenses, they are primarily motivated by a desire for violence, rather than a profit motive.

Skinheads account for large amounts of violence in comparison to their numbers. The Skinhead movement is growing in size and intensity, and it is collaborating with the KKK and other right wing extremists (Coplon, 1988). Leaders such as Tom Metzger and Richard Butler co-opt these young newcomers as "shock troopers" to advance their cause (ADL, 1990; Burden, 1992).

Tom Metzger stated, "Skinheads were born in violence. They're pissed off at the system. . . fighting every day" (Coplon, 1988, p. 58). Tom Metzger and the White Aryan Resistance have tried to use Metzger's son, John, and the Aryan Youth Movement to organize skinheads into one national organization, but have had limited success (Monitor, 1988).

Skinheads have done more than anything since the Order to popularize the far right movement. Skinhead violence, particularly in the northwest, became almost routine in the late 1980's (Martinez and Guinther, 1988).

Clark Martell, leader of Chicago Area Skinheads (CASH), also called Romantic Violence, described himself as a violent person, and said, "I love the white race and when you love something, you're the most vicious person on earth" (Coplon, 1988, p. 56). Skinheads operate in a manner similar to Nazi storm troopers and use some of the same dress and insignia (Coplon, 1988). Martell's group attends meetings at Robert Miles' farm and also promotes a white power rock group called "The Final Solution" (ADL, 1988a; 1987d). There are also other skinhead groups who promote their message through hard driving rock music (ADL, 1992).

RECRUITED BY OTHER RIGHT WING ORGANIZATIONS

Tom Metzger was recruiting skinheads very successfully in the west and Midwest. He had to curtail such public recruitment, however, after one of his WAR lieutenants visited skinheads who later beat a Portland, Oregon, Ethiopian student to death, Mulugeta Seraw. The Southern Poverty Law Center in Alabama successfully sued Metzger on vicarious liability principles and won a $12.5 million settlement for Seraw's family.

In contrast to Christian Identity's beliefs that blacks are "mud people" created in error on the third day, skinheads believe in

Odinism, worship of ancient Norse gods. They have similar white supremacist ideologies about "territorial imperative" carving an all-white enclave because of the expectation of an Armageddon-like racial holy war (VanBiema, 1993).

Skinhead violence accounted for twenty-two murders from 1990-93 with several persons awaiting trial. In 1992, skinheads were responsible for seven deaths, one quarter of all bias-related deaths that year in the United States. They appear to be more of a racist threat than the KKK. Besides the deaths is the way they terrorize the communities where they operate (VanBiema, 1993).

There is no central organization but many individual groups, operating much as other gangs, with some efforts at national organization. These include groups such as the Confederate Hammer Skins, Northern Hammer Skins, Chicago Area Skinheads, East Side White Pride, Fourth Reich Skinheads, Doc Marten Stompers, and American Front (see Appendix F). These groups have hooked up with the Klans, Aryan Nations, White Aryan Resistance, and Church of the Creator (ADL, 1992).

CHAPTER IX

Christian Identity Groups

Right wing extremists, unlike their left wing counterparts, are often not full-time extremists. Rather, they see themselves as "minutemen" ready at a moment's notice to fight for their rights as they see them (Hoffman, 1986). This is further borne out by the new citizen militias that began in the mid-1990's.

Right wing radicals have begun to participate in community activities and seek public support for their actions. Groups are switching to propaganda and political action. This is a perfect setting for the Identity Church movement, with its pseudo-theological racist movement, unaffiliated with any denomination, with supremacists teaching that Jews are the devil's children and blacks are "mud people" (Salholz and Miller, 1988).

There are numerous groups laying claims to the Christian Identity movement, with probable connections between many of them (see Appendix G). The Order; the Covenant, the Sword, and the Arm of the Lord (CSA); Aryan Nations; Posse Comitatus; and Christian Patriots are probably the best known of the groups centering around this movement. These groups involve paramilitary activity, tax protest, and religious convictions. Members are told they must endure dire events and prepare by taking military and survival training and stockpiling weapons and food (Ostfing, 1986).

Gordon Kahl, a Posse Comitatus member who shot two federal marshals, first brought the Christian Identity movement to widespread public attention. Christian Identity is neither a single organization nor a monolithic doctrine, but is, rather, hundreds of small groups dotted across the map nationwide. It should be looked at as a movement rather than a specific denomination or theology (Zeskind, 1987a).

The Identity movement has been in some disarray due to arrests of key leaders, including Richard Butler, Robert Miles, and Louis Beam, and the demise of Robert Mathews and the Order (Suall and Lowe, 1987). Butler, Miles, and Beam were among those indicted in April 1987 by a Fort Smith, Arkansas, grand jury on charges of seditious conspiracy. The defendants were later acquitted. Since then, Miles' death has lost the movement one of its thinkers.

IDENTITY THEOLOGY

Christian Identity was formalized by Edward Hine, an Englishman, who outlined the theory in an 1871 book, *Identification of The British Nations with Lost Israel*. This book theorized that today's Anglo-Saxon-Teuton whites are descendants of the lost tribes of Biblical Israelites, making white Christians the true people of the covenant (Flynn and Gerhardt, 1989).

The Identity movement is rooted in this Anglo-Israelism, which identified Anglo-Saxons with the Ten Lost Tribes of Israel. Its basis is that white Anglo-Saxons, not the Jewish people, are the chosen people of God. The Ten Lost tribes are the real predecessors of Nordic, British, and American whites, according to the theology. In other words, the United States is God's promised land and modern Israel is a hoax.

American Christian Identity has added its own features, in that it believes nonwhite races are pre-Adamic, God having created subhuman non-whites and set them outside the Garden of Eden before he created Adam and Eve. Then, Eve was implanted with two seeds, Abel and the white race having come from Adam's seed and the wicked Cain from the seed of the serpent Satan. This angered God who threw Adam, Eve, and the serpent out of the Garden, and decreed eternal racial conflict. Cain killed Abel and ran off to join the non-whites in the jungle (Ridgeway, 1990; Finch, 1983).

Finch (1983, p. 73) lists seven themes common to Identity sermons and thoughts:

(1) Identity believers see themselves as the last embattled few who will remain faithful through adversity, the "Remnants," the 144,000 stalwarts who preserve the faith and kingdom during the Tribulations in the Book of Revelations.

(2) There is a distinction between God's absolute law and man's faulty regulations. This justifies civil disobedience and rebellion to laws that do not agree with God's law.

(3) An assumption that this nation has flouted God's law and has thereby moved to the brink of disaster. Identity believers see an epochal cataclysm coming soon, pointing to high interest rates, crime and national disaster as signs of the disaster coming. This allows them to believe they do not owe allegiance to institutions corrupt enough to deserve God's wrath.

(4) The conviction that the white race in its present state is reduced from a higher glory, while other races were created as subservient physical beings who can rise no higher.

(5) An assumption that Jews are inherently evil, with cunning and a sense of purpose beyond normal human capacity, part of God's plan with the Jews a national enemy of white Christians.

(6) A belief that Jews create friction in the midst of white Christians to lead listeners to conclude that Jews must be removed from the earth to end this conflict.

(7) A promise that white Christian America will have no distinction in race, religion, and nationality. The movement offers theological rationalizations for racial and religious bigotry, and Identity groups include some of the most militant right wing extremists in th country. The late Wesley Swift was Identity's best known advocate after World War II. He was replaced by Richard Girnt Butler, who established the Church of Jesus Christ-Christian and the Aryan Nations (Suall and Lowe, 1987). Many Christian Identity followers believe that the era of the beast is fast approaching and that the field of Armageddon is in Nebraska or Kansas (Flynn and Gerhardt, 1989; ADL, 1983).

Richard Butler of the Aryan Nations, Robert Miles of the Mountain Church, Louis Beam of the KKK and Aryan Nations, and Robert Mathews of the Order were among the best known of those with Christian Identity philosophy. The Identity movement encompasses numerous small congregations, many of them with connections to the larger groups (see Appendix G).

RICHARD BUTLER AND THE ARYAN NATIONS

Richard Girnt Butler, born February 23, 1918, in Bennet, Colorado, is the best known Identity leader for his role with the Aryan Nations. Butler's group includes members of various other far-right groups, such as the various Ku Klux Klans, Posse, and neo-Nazi groups. He might well be considered in the "neo-Nazi" section or even as a hybrid group. He is being included with Christian Identity groups because that is how he primarily identifies and because of his religious connections not seen with the neo-Nazi groups. His mentor was the late Wesley Swift, who indoctrinated him into Christian Identity philosophy.

Active membership in the organization has been somewhat restricted for two reasons. First the group is so remote geographically that supporters may find it difficult to move there. Secondly, the members are required to tithe their earnings. Publications are *Calling Our Nation* and *Aryan Nations Newsletter* (George and Wilcox, 1992).

Butler headed the Christian Defense League of Swift's Anglo-Saxon Christian Congregation. Swift died in 1970 and Butler took over his role, although there were objections from William Potter Gale of the Posse Comitatus. After briefly aligning his church with the Louisiana-based National Emancipation of Our White Seed in 1976, Butler went on to form the Aryan Nations (ADL, 1988a).

Butler established his Church of Jesus Christ-Christian, which he says is a continuation of Wesley Swift's church, at Hayden Lake, Idaho, in the early 1970's and his compound there in 1974. It sits at the end of a road going through Coeur D'Alene National Forest in Kootenai County. The main gate is checked by men dressed in stromtrooper uniforms, with other patrolling the perimeter with attack dogs, while yet another watches from a guard tower (Vaughn, 1985).

Butler established the Aryan Nations as the political and paramilitary arm of the Church (Flynn and Gerhardt, 1989). He has played host to professional extremists from all over the country at his compound at annual conferences which allowed for various radicals to air their views and seek support.

Butler's theology combines a hatred of the Jewish and black people with visions of an impending apocalypse. His group advocates, and sometimes practices, armed violence to achieve its goals (Ostfing, 1986). The Aryan Nations acts as an umbrella group for many violent right wing radical groups (see Appendix H). The Aryan Nations militantly promotes anti-Semitism, white supremacy, and a white separatist state.

Aryan Nations publications spell out the fate of "race-traitors" who shall suffer the extreme penalty when lawful government is restored. Aryan Warriors can have no greater glory than to die like Bob Mathews of the Order, a martyr in the holy war against Satan and his agents, blacks, other non-white minorities, federal officers, tax collectors, and the media, all under control of the Jews (Vaughn, 1985).

Richard Butler has always been involved in the right wing movement as a "career extremist," always in a leadership role. Although he was at an age for retirement for many at the birth of the Order, he was still very active in a leadership role and provided a base of support for many of the players.

The first Aryan Nations World Congress was held in 1979, to encourage those with similar views to come together. The 1983 Aryan Nations World Congress at the Aryan Nations compound praised Gordon Kahl of the Posse Comitatus and called him a martyr for his death at the hands of the police. At the 1986 conference, a person calling himself "Daniel Johnson" tried to peddle his "Pace Amendment" which would mandate deportation of all non-white citizens from the United States (Suall and Lowe, 1987; ADL, 1987b). William Pierce of the National Alliance emerged from his compound in the West Virginia mountains to attend the 1995 Aryan Nations World Congress, the first time he attended this kind of a meeting in many years, possibly to explore how he could exert his control over national affairs of those groups in attendance.

Louis Beam, former Texas Klan leader, was the heir apparent when Richard Butler was charged by a Fort Smith grand jury (*Time*, 1987a). Beam had been Ambassador-at-Large for the Aryan Nations and was included in the Fort Smith indictment, along with Butler, for participating in a seditious conspiracy to overthrow the government. Butler's ministry also has connections with the Aryan Brotherhood, a prison white supremacist group that has operated since the 1960's. Aryan Nations sends out two prison publications, *Calling Our Nation* and *The Way* (ADL, 1988a). The prison ministry is led by Jane Housell.

The Aryan Nations has attracted fanatical members, such as those in the Order. It has come under constant government surveillance (George and Wilcox, 1992). In October 1986, four bombs were set off in the town of Coeur d'Alene, Idaho, to divert attention from a bank robbery that never took place. Several of those arrested were Aryan Nations members (ADL, 1988a).

Also, in 1986, the Aryan Nations World Congress attracted many participants, including Thomas G. Harrelson, who had joined the Aryan Nations through a prison ministry while serving time for bank robbery. After a bank robbery in Illinois and an attack on a police chief, he was placed on the FBI's Ten Most Wanted List. He was apprehended, pled guilty, and sentenced to five years in prison (ADL, 1988a).

When Butler was battling his seditious conspiracy indictment, Kim Badynski of the Northwest Knights of the KKK, was involved in efforts to raise money for his defense. Badynski was appointed security chief of the Aryan Nations. Charles and Betty Tate, parents of David Tate, of the Order, were in charge of printing operations. Larry McCurry and Carl Franklin were named Identity ministers (ADL, 1988a).

ROBERT MILES

Robert Miles, former KKK Grand Dragon, then the leader of the Mountain Church of Jesus Christ in Cohoctaw, Michigan, and now deceased, was long an educated speaker for the right wing movement. Miles was another principal of the Aryan Nations and Identity movement, operating the Mountain Church or Mountain Kirk in Cohoctaw, Michigan. He also ran a prison ministry from there.

Miles, one of the clearest thinkers on the violent edge of the racist movement, was instrumental in bringing together different Ku Klux Klan and neo-Nazi leaders. His version of Identity theology was called "Dualism," which differs somewhat from Identity philosophy, but was close enough for Richard Butler and other Identity ministers to be comfortable with it (Flynn and Gerhardt, 1989; Suall and Lowe, 1987).

Miles advocated a "10% Solution" which would mean setting aside the five states of the Pacific northwest for a White Aryan Republic. Southern extremists were not favorable to this solution. This Northwest Territorial Imperative has been endorsed by the Knights of the KKK from Tuscumbia and key activists have moved to the area (ADL, 1988a).

Miles was a featured speaker at meetings of the Covenant, the Sword, and the Arm of the Lord (CSA) as well as meetings of the Christian Patriots Defense League. He was Midwest coordinator for the Aryan Nations. He was also a star at the 1988 sedition trail at Fort Smith, where he and the others were acquitted. Newspaper reports of the trial described testimony by CSA leader James Ellison who turned state's evidence. Ellison testified that Miles and Richard Butler discussed polluting water supplies of large cities to show that the government was powerless and cause revolution among the people. Cyanide would be used as Miles had given Ellison about 200 pounds of the chemical in September 1981. Ellison said, "Mr. Miles said it would kill a lot of people, and the ones it would kill, it wouldn't really matter. It would be a good cleansing" (ADL, 1988a, p. 132).

Robert Miles developed an idea in 1987 of "leaderless cells," an organizational structure of small autonomous groups. This would effectively thwart infiltration and defuse culpability. He compared the idea to a spider web. When you put your hand in it, it gives, but is still there when you remove your hand (Smo-lowe, 1995). This idea probably goes back to the original Minutemen and their "secret cells" and the small breakoff cells that spun away when the Order was terminated. In 1990, Miles ceased publishing his magazine, *From the Mountain*, due to his wife's ill health (George and Wilcox, 1992).

Robert Miles typified the "career extremist" of the typology, acting as a "charismatic leader" for the cause. He was more intellectual than most of the right wing leaders and was able to provide a sound theological basis for the various types of followers in his movement. Although Miles died before the citizen militias hit the national news, his legacy of organizing groups and providing a theology and platform continues.

The white Christian Republic would be the Aryan Nations homeground. Members of different Klan factions, the White Aryan Resistance, neo-Nazi groups, the Posse, and other groups all consider themselves to be part of the umbrella group of the Aryan Nations (Zeskind, 1987b).

ROBERT JAY MATHEWS: THE ORDER

Robert Jay Mathews was born in Marfa, Arizona, on January 6, 1953. He died December 8, 1984, on Whidbey Island, in Puget Sound, Washington, in pursuit of the Silent Brotherhood and his dream of a white American homeland. Mathews began the Sons of Liberty in the Arizona desert in 1972 and had previously been a member of the John Birch Society. He proposed a White American Bastion, by which whites would migrate to the Pacific northwest, and he continued this designation throughout the reign of the Order. The Order was a terrorist group which sought to bankroll this new white American homeland (Flynn and Gerhardt, 1989).

Mathews was an active and influential recruiter for the National Alliance. He recruited members for the Order from the National Alliance, Aryan Nations, and Klan groups, many of the members also being Christian Identity followers.

The Order's first act after its October 1983 birth was a robbery involving World Wide Video. This was the beginning of the most profitable crime spree in U. S. history. It was also the first organized effort in this century by a right wing group to over-throw the U. S. government. Mathews made up a hit list which did not include blacks, whom he did not see as a major problem, but did include prominent Jews and government officials (Martinez and Guinther, 1988; ADL 1985b).

Bob Mathews issued a declaration of war at the inception of the Order and had a medallion struck for the members (Martinez and Guinther, 1988). Using the typology developed, Mathews was clearly a leader fulfilling the needs of his followers to be recognized, to be part of a closeknit group, and to support a cause. He was an ace recruiter for this violent terrorist group, variously called the Order, the Silent Brotherhood, and the Bruder Schweigen.

Mathews carefully planned his crusade and made efforts to recruit people with various specialties and used a variety of methods to recruit people, including putting advertisements in magazines. His ingenuity did not end with recruiting practices but continued into his security practices. Members of the Order used code names and aliases (see Appendix I). For instance, Mathews used "Carlos" after the international assassin (Flynn and Gerhardt, 1989).

Mathews married Debbie McGarrity, who answered his *Mother Earth News* advertisement. Ken Loff, a charter member of the group, and code named "Marbles," was Mathews' next door neighbor, and became involved in his teachings and beliefs. He was recruited to be the organization's banker and was to keep the money at his farm near Ione, Washington. Charles Ostrout, who provided inside information on the Brinks robbery, was a mail room supervisor who answered his advertisement for the White American Bastion. Ostrout, in turn, recruited his supervisor, Ronald King (Flynn and Gerhardt, 1989).

Core membership came from the Aryan Nations, the Covenant, the Sword, and the Arm of the Lord (CSA), and the Ku Klux Klans (see Appendix I). Start-up money came from a counterfeit operation associated with the Aryan Nations and from a series of armored car and bank robberies (Martinez and Guinther, 1988).

Andrew Virgil Barnhill, "Mr. Closet," field commander, and Randall Rader, "Field Marshall" or "Big Boy," expert in paramilitary training, came from the CSA, as well as Richard Scutari, "Joshua" or "Mr. Black," who was recruited for his martial arts expertise. Scutari was later sought in connection with the Brinks car robbery. He was also indicted and acquitted of involvement in the Alan Berg murder. He was one of the twelve signing the Declaration of War. He pled guilty to racketeering, conspiracy to racketeer, and to his part in the Brinks robbery. He was sentenced to sixty years in prison (ADL, 1988a).

Ardie McBrearty, of the Posse Comitatus, was a financial expert and an expert in voice stress analysis, talents which likely were the reason for his code name, "Learned Professor." Robert Merki, "Noah," and his wife, Sharon, "Mother Goose" or "Mrs. God," connected with Mathews through an Identity church member (Flynn and Gerhard, 1989). The Merkis were previously experienced counterfeiters (Coates, 1987).

Jim Dye, "Mr. May," came from the KKK and then the National Alliance, where Thomas Martinez introduced him to Mathews. Martinez later helped the FBI bring down the Order as an FBI informant (Flynn and Gerhardt, 1989).

Zillah Craig became Mathews' lover and later bore his child. It was Craig's mother, Jean Craig, "Rainey," who helped set up the Alan Berg murder by masquerading as a fan and doing intelligence work to learn the pattern of his activities. Jean Craig and Richard Scutari were acquitted of this murder, but Bruce Carroll Pierce and David Lane were each sentenced to one hundred fifty years in prison (ADL, 1988a). Bruce Pierce has nearly twenty aliases, including "Logan" and "Brigham."

David E. Lane, "Lone Wolf," had long been involved with extremist groups, including the KKK and neo-Nazi groups. He had previously been involved with the Aryan Nations and Pierce was deeply into the right wing extremist movement and was connected with *The Primrose and Cattleman's Gazette.* Lane joined Bob Mathews and the Order in 1983 and was allegedly involved in the $3.6 million Brinks robbery in Ukiah, California. He was convicted of racketeering charges and of violating Alan Berg's civil rights for which he was sentenced to 150 years in prison (ADL, 1988a).

David Tate was a previous chief of security for the Aryan Nations and had been in charge of training members for hand-to-hand combat. He was also connected to Gayman's Identity Church, the Church of Israel. Gary Yarbrough, "Yosemite Sam" or "Reds," another Aryan Nations security chief, had been recruited for that movement by Richard Butler through his prison ministry while Yarbrough was in an Arizona prison (Coates, 1987). When FBI agents showed up to arrest Yarbrough's brother, Steven, Gary Yarbrough opened fire on three FBI agents with a .45 caliber handgun. The submachine gun used to kill Alan Berg was later found in a search of the residence. Yarbrough was later captured after they found him with Bob Mathews in Portland, Oregon. Mathews escaped that encounter (ADL, 1988a).

Mathews' group became bolder and began to stockpile weapons and establish special paramilitary cells, which would break off, each with its own leader, if the group were to fall. This happened after the group's demise and these secret cells and their members were mostly not identified after they went underground.

Mathews set up the Mountain Man Supply Company, which purchased over 137 shipments of military gear and ammunition. He also acquired supplies from other sources. The major source of illegal weapons for terrorists is the United States government, in the form of equipment stolen from military bases. Right wing extremist groups have taken advantage of this supply source (Martinez and Guinther, 1988).

Previously, Mathews was the western recruiter for William Pierce's National Alliance. Mathews apparently fashioned the Order after *The Turner Diaries*, which was written by William Pierce under the pseudonym Andrew Macdonald. Mathews told an informant that the revolution portrayed in *The Turner Diaries* had begun. During the reign of the Order, they committed three murders, including Jewish talk show host Alan Berg, bombed an Idaho synagogue, heisted an armored car for $3.6 million, which was distributed to various hate groups, and had a shootout with police, which led to Mathews' death. Most of the Order's members are serving lengthy prison terms (Suall and Lowe, 1987; ADL, 1988a).

Federal and state officials located Mathews and his associates on Whidbey Island in December 1984, where Mathews had rented three residences and had large caches of weapons. Order members were arrested, including Robert and Sharon Merki, the two of them on counterfeiting charges. Mathews' residence was surrounded and he sent out Ian Stewart, Sharon Merki's son, with a canvas bag containing $40,000. Negotiations failed as did attempts to enter the residence with covering gunfire. Illumination flares were dropped by a helicopter overhead and the house went up in flames, ending the reign of the Order. Mathews became a martyr for the right wing.

Thirty-eight members of the Order were prosecuted. These included those convicted of murdering Alan Berg (Salholz and Miller, 1988) and David Tate for murdering a Missouri state trooper. Authorities stopped Mathews four months short of attempting a shutdown of a major U. S. city through terrorism (Flynn and Gerhardt, 1989).

FBI infiltration of the Order caused the extremists continuing problems. Eugene Kinerk of the Aryan Nations became an FBI informant and provided an Aryan Nations membership list before committing suicide. Gary Yarbrough and Robert Bowyer of the Aryan Nations and Elden "Bud" Cutler, who succeeded Yarbrough as security chief for the Aryan Nations, were arrested for trying to hire an undercover FBI agent to decapitate Thomas Martinez after his role as an FBI informant was revealed (Martinez and Guinther, 1988).

The incarceration of the Order's members and death of its leader does not mean it was completely neutralized. There are indications that throughout 1984 and 1985, members were busy establishing a network of safehouses and support cells in the southwest and southeast regions of the United States. The organization of the group was such that the identity of many members still at large was not known (Hoffman, 1986).

The Order provides a good test of the categories listed in the typology because the Order was such a varied group. The Order had a career extremist as its leader, Bob Mathews. There were dedicated followers, such as his next door neighbor, Ken Loff, Zillah Craig, his lover, and Ardie McBrearty, a long time Posse member. There were the dispossessed, such as Thomas Martinez, who later became an FBI informant. Martinez saw himself losing his job and his future, which went to minorities, and became engrossed in the movement. There were hard core criminals, such as Gary Yarbrough, who was recruited while still in prison. There were those who were thrill seekers, such as Richie Kemp, whose code name went from "Jolly" for the Jolly Green Giant to "Hammer" after he murdered a man with a hammer because he thought he was an informant, and apparently enjoyed his work (Martinez and Guinther, 1988).

POSSE COMITATUS

The Posse Comitatus is an Identity organization composed of loosely affiliated bands of armed vigilantes and survivalists that began in 1969 (see Appendix J). Henry L. (Mike) Beach, a former 1930's "Silver Shirt," and retired Army Colonel William Potter Gale, founded the Posse. While some Nazi groups had German roots, the Silver Shirts with which Beach had been associated were of predominantly American stock (Strong, 1941). Beach has since distanced himself from the group (ADL, 1988a).

The Posse Comitatus is unified only in general principle. It is a loose confederation of several groups. Most members are likely to support the principles and likely belong to other groups, such as tax protestors and gun control opponents (Finch, 1983).

Gale also identified with Richard Butler and the Aryan Nations and has his own Identity Church, the Ministry of Christ Church, in Mariposa, California. Several Posse members have gone on to form their own churches. Gale was sentenced to federal prison for a year and a day in January 1988. He died on April 28, 1988 at the age of seventy-one (ADL, 1988a).

Gale had organized the paramilitary California Rangers in 1960. He was an early "Identity leader." His association with Richard Butler led to Butler being introduced to the Identity movement. He was also associated with the Christian Conservative Churches of America. He helped found the Posse and was instrumental in the founding of the Committee of The States.

The Posse Comitatus is a politically motivated organization famous for its threats against the establishment brand of justice and those who enforce it, namely police officers, especially federal officers. The Kansas Bureau of Investigation estimated Posse membership at 2.5 million members in the early 1980's. It is not possible to estimate membership now due to secrecy. The Posse makes no secret of gun ownership by its members, but evidence of whether or not members are training as a military style group has not shown up. The Posse members are wary of attention, but there have been reports of them training secretly (Finch, 1983).

The Posse is said to have connections to the Church of Jesus Christ-Christian, Richard Butler's Aryan Nations alterego (Remesch-Allnut, 1985). Posse Comitatus groups have stockpiled sophisticated weapons, replacing the Minutemen of the 1960's (Flynn and Gerhardt, 1989).

Jim Wickstrom became a spokesman for the Posse and published a newsletter, *The Posse Noose,* making inflammatory statements. Wickstrom was jailed in March 1984, charged with bail jumping and impersonating a public official. The Posse had formed its own township of a couple of a dozen mobile homes near Tigerton, Wisconsin, Wickstrom's hometown, and called it "Tigerton Dells." Wickstrom named himself municipal judge and town clerk and thereby incurred the charges of impersonating a public official (George and Wilcox, 1992). Posse Comitatus is Latin for "power of the county" and the Posse literally believes that all governmental power rests at the county level. Posse member Gordon Kahl brought the Posse to national attention when he killed two federal marshals and his son was badly wounded in a shootout in North Dakota in 1983. Kahl later died in another shootout with police in which an Arkansas sheriff was killed (Suall and Lowe, 1987).

Publications exhort farmers to stop paying taxes, ignore state and federal judicial authority, stop using U. S. currency, and to arm themselves. The Posse Comitatus has also stated in its publications that abortion is part of the global conspiracy "masterminded" by the Jews (Hoffman, 1986). Posse members have gone from common law nuisance suits to selling 50-cent licenses for unlimited access to public lands. They have harassed and assaulted officials and Posse members have been sent to prison in some cases.

Until Gordon Kahl, the Posse had managed to keep itself out of public view and urged followers to keep their membership secret. From time to time, however, Posse clashes with the courts and government are reported. Donald Minniecheske was pastor of the Life Science Church in Tigerton Dells, Wisconsin, and claimed that his church was exempt from paying taxes. The church attracted members of the Posse, which the news article about this incident called a white supremacist, anti-Semitic group advocating arming in self defense and opposing federal tax laws. A federal judge disagreed that the Life Science church in this case was tax exempt and sold land and property that were part of the Posse Comitatus compound (*Chicago Tribune*, August 30, 1993).

OTHER IDENTITY GROUPS
The Covenant, the Sword, and the Arm of the Lord

The Covenant, the Sword, and the Arm of the Lord (CSA) is a paramilitary survivalist group which has operated a settlement, Identity-style, on 224 acres of ground near the Arkansas-Missouri border (ADL, 1988a). Jim Ellison, along with his second in command, Kerry Noble, led the Covenant, the Sword, and the Arm of the Lord (CSA), which was aligned with Christian Identity groups. Kerry Noble explained his group as being Christian survivalists preparing for the ultimate holocaust. The CSA practiced Identity theology. They taught "Endtimer Overcomer Survival Training" to members and non-members in urban warfare, weaponry, and survivalism. After the Order was quashed, officers of the Bureau of Alcohol, Tobacco, and Firearms (BATF), entered Ellison's CSA compound, called Zarepath-Horeb, on the Missouri-Arkansas border, in April 1985, and found an arsenal of deadly weapons and explosives. This included thirty gallons of poisonous cyanide, and a shop where automatic weapons were manufactured. Ellison was convicted on charges of criminal racketeering that included arson and bombing charges. Other members were also in prison, making the future of the group shaky (Suall and Lowe, 1987; ADL, 1988a).

Ellison testified in federal court that the thirty gallons of cyanide came from Robert Miles, who said that it would kill a lot of people. Ellison further testified that Miles later visited the compound and discussed using the cyanide to poison the water supplies of New York City and Washington, D.C., for a "good cleansing" (Bishop, 1988).

CHRISTIAN PATRIOTS DEFENSE LEAGUE

John R. (Johnny Bob) Harrell was a former real estate and mausoleum salesman who turned to religion and conservative politics after a miraculous recovery from lymph cancer in 1959. He had some supporters living on the grounds of his estate in Flora, Illinois. He went into hiding with his family after troubles with the IRS and an indictment for hiding a military deserter . He later served four years in federal prison and after his probation ended in 1976, he formed the Christian Patriots Defense League (Finch, 1983).

The Christian Patriots Defense League (CPDL) began in 1976 as a new hate group (Suall and Lowe, 1987). Its publication is the *Paul Revere Club Newsletter.* The Christian Patriots acted as a central organization of the Christian Identity or patriot movement, being an extreme right wing "survivalist" group engaging in paramilitary training. Harrell still heads the group, which emerged from his earlier group, the Christian Conservative Churches of America. Hard to believe, Harrell actually formed several groups, operating together, including the Christian Patriots Defense League, the Citizens Emergency Defense System, the Paul Revere Club and the Save America Gun Club, with some serving fund raising and some political purposes (Finch, 1983).

In 1979, Harrell proclaimed CPDL's purpose was to awaken and organize patriots who are striving against the international Jewish conspiracy which hates Christ, against Communism, gun control, and taxation. The Christian Patriots Defense League practices racism and is anti-Semitic at its base. Harrell advocated "defense posts" which would be regional rallying points and safety locations for these patriots (ADL, 1988a). Colonel Gordon "Jack" Mohr (U. S. Army Retired), a one-time lecturer for the John Birch Society, as well as Ret. U. S. Army Col. B. F. VonStahl, served as military advisors. Harrell was also closely connected to the CSA and their survival and paramilitary school

(Finch, 1983). Mohr also headed Harrell's Citizen's Emergency Defense System.

The survivalist and paramilitary training stem from the Identity belief that the present structure of this country will collapse, and this will culminate in racial conflict for which white Americans must prepare. Harrell sponsored the Freedom Festival, which began in 1971, and was then held in Flora, Illinois, at Harrell's fifty-five acre estate. Harrell was forced to desist from paramilitary training in 1986 and the size of the Festival diminished (ADL, 1988a). Harrell has since relocated.

ARIZONA PATRIOTS

Former screen star Ty Hardin led the Arizona Patriots, an Identity group with Posse-like activities until he moved to California and they regrouped (Suall and Lowe, 1987). In 1984, the Arizona Patriots showed their disagreement with the normal democratic process when members issued an "indictment" against all Arizona elected officials, charging them with violations of their oaths of office and the U. S. Constitution. Eight Patriots were indicted in 1986 for various crimes including a plot to finance a paramilitary base by robbing an armored car in Nevada, and plans to bomb a synagogue in Phoenix and an IRS facility in Utah. Several members, when arrested, had blueprints to electrical systems of two major cities and the piping system for a third (Martinez and Guinther, 1988; ADL, 1988a).

COMMITTEE OF THE STATES

Closely connected to the Patriots is the Committee of the States, of Nevada, whose members were connected to the crimes committed by the Arizona Patriots (Suall and Lowe, 1987; Flynn and Gerhardt, 1989). The Committee is a right wing extremist tax protest group formed July 4, 1984, in Mariposa, California. Its name comes from the Articles of Confederation, predecessor to the U. S. Constitution, which called for a Committee of the States to run the country. This group has also served "indictments" on members of Congress.

William Potter Gale, besides his Posse connections, led the Committee of the States. He was also an Identity minister and was among those indicted for the Patriots' violent acts. The committee was formed in Mariposa, California, in 1984 (ADL, 1988a). The organization is also called the Committee of the States in Congress Assembled and subscribes to the ideals of the Posse Comitatus (ADL, 1987c).

CHURCH OF CHRIST

Pete Peters pastors the Church of Christ, an Identity church in LaPorte, Colorado, near Fort Collins. He edits *Scriptures for America*, advocating Identity theology against blacks and Jews. His feud with Alan Berg over Berg's inflammatory radio commentaries may have contributed to Berg's death at the hands of the Order. Zillah Craig met David Lane at this church and through Lane, she met Robert Mathews. Robert and Sharon Merki also met Mathews through church members (Flynn and Gerhardt, 1989). Peters' ministry is patterned after the late Sheldon Emry's Lord's Covenant Church. Several members of the Order attended Pete Peters church (ADL, 1989).

LORD'S COVENANT CHURCH or AMERICA'S PROMISE

Sheldon Emry was a well-known Identity sage from Prescott, Arizona, until his death in 1985. Emry conducted "America's Promise" radio program and was a longtime Identity proponent and hater of Jews (ADL, 1988a). His death was a setback for the Identity movement because of his well known radio ministry. Emry headed the Phoenix-based Lord's Covenant Church, also called America's Promise (ADL, 1988b). This Church netted half a million dollars a year with their radio ministry (Flynn and Gerhardt, 1989). Emry was also active with the Citizen's Emergency Defense System and Christian Patriots Defense League. Ben Williams led the group after Emry's death until Williams established his own ministry, America's Covenant Church. Rev. Dave Barley then took over (ADL, 1988a).

CHURCH OF ISRAEL

Dan Gayman leads the Church of Israel, originally called Church of our Christian Heritage, in Schell City, Missouri. Gayman's church was named by a Fort Smith grand jury as the recipient of $10,000 seized by the Order. Gayman's church consists of half a dozen buildings on 123 acres with forty to sixty followers at any given time. David Tate, serving life for murdering a Missouri state trooper, was reportedly a member of this church (Flynn and Gerhardt, 1989).

Dan Gayman was a former Missouri high school principal. He preaches from the pulpit and travels across the country on speaking tours. He also delivers printed materials and cassette tapes. He goes beyond denying Jews are the Chosen People and tries to prove that Jews are "Satan's seed." He has been a leading figure in the Identity movement for several years. He was also affiliated with the groups National Emancipation of Our White Seed, the Christian Defense League and James K. Warren, and the New Christian Crusade Church, as well as Aryan Nations groups. He has been editor of *Zion's Watchman*, a national Identity monthly magazine. He spoke at the 1979 Aryan Nations Conference, calling himself an "Identity Bishop." (ADL, 1988a).

SWORD OF CHRIST

Ralph P. Forbes was once George Lincoln Rockwell's "captain" and is the prime mover in the Sword of Christ Good News Ministry of London, Arkansas. The group is active in the anti-Semitic movement, the Identity movement, and in the Liberty-Lobby operated Populist Party. Forbes has run for public offices several times. He has applied for and been denied a nonprofit mailing permit for his publication *Good News America*.

THE DUCK CLUBS

Robert White decided to save American in the summer of 1980 and produced a large patriotic magazine laced with conspiracy theories and doomsday news. It featured a comical duck defending the Panama Canal, flying a B-1 bomber. The duck became a symbol and people paid a $10 subscription for the *Duck Club Magazine*, with a goal of one million subscribers, the money to be used in the 1982 elections to elect conservative candidates. White encouraged local chapters of the "Duck Club" (Finch, 1983).

The "Duck Club" is one of several "patriot" organizations operating in the northwest. This group came to attention when a member of the Seattle Club, Donald Rice, bludgeoned to death four members of the Goldmark family because he mistakenly thought they were Jewish. Rice was a follower of Jack Mohr and thought killing the family was his patriotic duty. Mohr leads the Christian Emergency Defense Fund of Mississippi and is a charismatic and popular speaker that Identity followers travel hundreds of miles to hear (ADL, 1988a).

CHURCH OF THE CREATOR

Ben Klassen emigrated to the United States from the Ukraine by way of Mexico and then Canada. He is a retired real estate salesman and ran for office and was elected to the Florida State Legislature in 1966, campaigning against busing and the federal government. He was active in the John Birch Society and ran one of their bookstores, the American Opinion Bookstore. He fell out with the Society over who was controlling the conspiracy to overthrow the United States.

Klassen founded the Church of the Creator in Lighthouse Point, Florida, in 1973, with anti-Jewish and white supremacy messages. He has published several books, including *The White Man's Bible*, and other anti-Jewish and racist materials. He left Florida in 1982 with construction of a new church, the Church of the Creator, in Mulberry, a mountainous area of western North Carolina. In 1983, publication began of an anti-Semitic white racist tabloid, *Racial Loyalty* (ADL, 1988a).

In 1993, suspects aligned with the Church of the Creator in Florida, members of Tom Metzger's White Aryan Resistance, and the Fourth Reich skinheads plotted to bomb a prominent black church in Los Angeles. This was to be the beginning of an attempt to provoke an all-out race war (Monroe, 1993).

OTHER GROUPS

Elohim City is another remote Identity camp on the Oklahoma-Arkansas border, led by Rev. Robert Millar, who has CSA ties. The thirty-five to forty residents are sometimes armed (ADL, 1988a). There are numerous other small Identity churches, many in the Pacific northwest. This usually involves a single Pastor and weekly services (Flynn and Gerhardt, 1989).

Republic v. Democracy is another Christian Patriots organization lead by Robert Wangrud of Oregon City, Oregon. It is small, overtly racist, and its newsletter, *Behold*, is edited by Aryan Nations leader Ed Arlt (ADL, 1988a). Republic v. Democracy promotes the idea that the Constitution itself is a racist document, and that only white people should be allowed to be citizens of the United States. They believe that the proper form of government allowed by the Constitution is a "republic" governed by "white law" (CDR, 1988).

The American Pistol and Rifle Association bills itself as similar to the National Rifle Association but with a more grass roots emphasis. It is into survivalism, food storage, and managing during times of civil disorder. It is of interest because Virgil Barnhill is involved with it. He is the father of Andrew Barnhill, charter member of the Order. The senior Barnhill went on to become a member of the ultra-conservative Florida Patriots, gun control enemies (Flynn and Gerhardt, 1989). Another more hard core alternative to the NRA is the National Association to Keep and Bear Arms (NAKBA). Its publication is the *Armed Citizen News*. NAKBA promotes the John Birch Society and Liberty Lobby.

The largest Christian Patriots organization in the northwest is the Populist Party which reorganized in 1987 to try and make a comeback. George Hansen, a former Idaho Congressman, and David Duke, former Knights of the KKK Imperial Wizard, proclaimed their membership and their willingness to run for office on this ticket (ADL, 1988a; CDR, 1988). Other Christian Patriot and Identity groups are tax protestors, fight against gun control, and some have as their emphasis the fight to take away Native American treaty rights (ADL, 1988a).

Groups billing themselves as Family Farm Preservation and using "Fractional Reserve Notes" as a takeoff to federal reserve notes, have come on the scene. Terry Nichols had already made a name for himself as an extremist in the courtroom before he was arrested in connection with the Oklahoma City bombing. He used "fractional reserve notes" to pay off his credit card debts.

The radical right is using "funny money" to create credit of their own to save themselves from financial ruin. Nichols said that the banks gave him credit and he was giving them credit, that banks cheat people out of their money by making loans and charging interest. Terry Nichols has been linked to the Family Farm Preservation and the Posse Comitatus. Family Farm Preservation leaders are under indictment for $65 million in bogus money orders. They are headquartered in Tigerton, Wisconsin, and Chief German of that police department said that the right wing extremists had gotten rid of their camos, stockpiled weapons, and set up offices (Day One, ABC, May 18, 1995).

Family Farm Preservation is not the first effort to take grass roots action to protect the midwest farmers from financial ruin. The National Agricultural Press Association is described as a "right wing extremist organization claiming more than 3,000 members in 30 states." It holds rallies and published the now defunct *Primrose and Cattleman's Gazette* with articles about the "Jewish question" and with advertisements from the Aryan Nations. It advised farmers to file lawsuits to nullify federal loans, claiming them to be illegal. The founder, Rick Elliot, was indicted for stealing money from its supporters (Encyclopedia of Associations, 1990, p. 13890).

The western states have also spawned another grassroots movement called the "Sagebrush Rebellion" which supports landowners' rights in the midwestern states. The Bureau of Land Management and Forest Service have come under attack by ranchers, farmers, and loggers fed up with federal rules about the use of their land, and about water rights and wildlife habitats. The Carson City Forest Rangers Office was bombed in March 1995 and rangers have become very cautious about services notices to landowners and have started traveling together. These local control activists have found a common cause with the new militias and land reform rebels have developed an appetite for the militia-style conspiracies. The "National Federal Lands Conference," one leading group, warns about the New World Order and United Nations in a fund raising letter (Smolowe, 1995).

Prior to these more recent lands rights' proponents, were groups springing up in the mid-1980's geared to deny native

Americans their treaty rights and property. Citizens Equal Rights Alliance of Big Arm, Montana, led a national drive. A local organization, All Citizens Equal (ACE) also worked against treaty rights (CDR, 1988).

CHAPTER X

The Militia Movement
Citizen Militias: The New Wave

The Mid-1990's, particularly 1994 and 1995, saw a new type of organization develop with informal branches all over the country. Many of them have some of the same principles, but the groups are generally without central organization. Some, however, do have branches in several states.

The new groups are billed as militias, patriots, or sometimes do not name themselves at the onset, possibly to attract new recruits without the stigma of one group or the other. For instance, a meeting was held in Benton, Illinois, in September 1994, after announcements had been passed out at a candidate's forum prior to the November 1994 election, and other places, inviting people to the meeting with the circular questioning "Are you wondering what's happening to your country? What's wrong? Who's causing it? Who's the enemy? Why is it happening? Why are they doing it? What can be done? What can I do?" No particular group was named as setting up the meeting, and the purpose of it was left somewhat ambiguous.

At the meeting in Benton, Illinois, flyers were passed out that warned of reflective stickers to guide NATO troops, searches without warrants, and the closing of military bases and reopening them to train foreign troops. Other flyers talked of the murder of members of the Weaver family by an FBI sniper and the biochip that is to be implanted into Americans for identification, maps of concentration camps, and the questionnaire that was circulated to U. S. Marines in the 29th Platoon in California in May 1994, asking them if they would fire on American troops.

The Resister, which is billed as the "Official Publication of the Special Forces Underground" was passed out with copies of that questionnaire. *The Resister* stated that the questionnaire was first given to operators by the commanders of SEAL Team Six on September 15, 1993 and to remaining SEAL platoons during September and October. Later, U. S. Army personnel were given the same questionnaire. *The Resister* states some of their goals in an open letter to "Dear Patriot," and gives their philosophy as strict constitutionalism, isolationism, laissez-faire capitalism, individual rights, limited government, and republicanism, the principles upon which this nation was founded. The publication states that what is opposed is statism, liberalism, tribalism, socialism, collectivism, internationalism, democracy, altruism, pull politics, and the New World Order. The opposition to democracy is stated to be because it is the "very antithesis of individual rights" and a suggestion is given to read the works of our Founding Father to get more eloquent arguments against democracy. There are various articles in this publication, several well written, grammatically correct, and using pseudonyms (*The Resister,* 1994).

Meeting such as the one in Benton, Illinois, have spawned some of the more recent militia and patriot groups. It is likely that groups in existence or at least collections of people have used such forums to express their ideas and gain enough support to organize a group that can carry forth their ideas.

Citizen militias are as old as our nation but very new to take a place in the right wing extremist movement. They vary from state to state and even county to county. Some are more militant than others. Glad Hall, head of the Southern Illinois Patriots League, new on the scene in 1995, stated "we advise everyone in our group to be as well armed as they can afford to be and possess as much ammunition as they can afford (Woolf, "Political Agenda," 4/30/95, 11a). Hall denied any connection with violence.

Loosely organized paramilitary groups of mostly white men are recruiting members, stockpiling weapons, and preparing for the worst they can imagine. This is the armed, military edge of a group of disgruntled citizens, often called "patriots" (see Appendix K). Members of the greater patriot movement feel wronged by the   government, and haunted by the economy, mistrusting anyone in power much more than the normal citizen and voter. The patriot groups are borne of fear and frustration. They claim to be different than other right wing groups such as the KKK and Posse Comitatus, pointing out a belief that the government is robbing them of inalienable rights, such as the right to bear arms. Some of the people emerging as militia leaders have ties with previous hate groups. Watch dog groups see the militias as a new way of window dressing the same old ideas.

BEWARE APRIL 19

April 19 is a special date to the new militias. They often point out the significance of that date. The Militia of Montana's March newsletter, *Taking Aim*, detailed the happenings on April 19 (Tharp, 1995). It was April 19, 1775, when the Battle of Lexington opened America's Civil War. On this same date in 1993, the siege of the Branch Davidian compound in Waco, Texas, ended. On April 19, 1995, Richard Wayne Snell, a member of the Covenant, the Sword, and the Arm of the Lord, was executed for the murder of a Jewish businessman and a black police officer. Tim McVeigh's forged South Dakota driver's license gave the date of issue for the fictional license as April 19, 1993, the date that ended the Waco siege (Gleick, May 1, 1995). It was April 19, 1995, also, when the bombing of the federal building in Oklahoma City brought disaster to the nation.

In the wake of the April 1995 Oklahoma City bombing of the Alfred P. Murrah Federal Building, Americans had to start looking at the streak of paranoia running through the country that looked at the federal government as the enemy. Sometimes even the more outrageous claims are spoken by people who are normally reasonable. Theories include Russian troops hidden in Detroit salt mines, secret highway markers to guide foreign troops (Farley, 1994), L. A. gangs helping the U. N. to disarm American, and Janet Reno being an agent of Jewish Columbian drug lords.

Conspiracy theories allow normally reasonable Americans to identify a culprit and have someone to blame. Most have roots in ideas such as the government plotting against its citizens, subverting and eliminating your local sheriff, training U. N. troops in this country, hiring Chinese police to disarm the American people, and monitoring people with sophisticated minute devices that are implanted (Levinson, 1995).

These new ranks of the right wing extremist movement contain quite a mixture of dissatisfied Americans. There are tax protestors, home schoolers, Christian fundamentalists and Constitutionalists who are concerned with legal protests against the government's activities. But, there are also the scattered neo-Nazis and white supremacists with paranoia and conspiracy theory binding the two elements together (Smolowe, 1995).

Some fairly reasonable people have come to view the government as their enemy because of understandable grievances about economic defeats in the1990's (Lacayo, 1995). Most of them are not violent, but they may become involved with groups who do not have their same non-violent orientation.

What binds these elements together is their great paranoia. Besides the other evidence they present for a conspiracy involving a United Nations invasion and one world government, they also believe that Soviet fighter jets are on standby in Biloxi, Mississippi; "black choppers" with no markings signal imminent occupation by armies of the one world government; and stickers on interstate highways are coded to direct the invading army (Smolowe, 1995).

MICHIGAN MILITIA

Norman Olson and Ray Southwell organized the Michigan Militia Corps in April 1994. They resigned their leadership positions in April 1995 after publicizing theories about the Oklahoma City bombing that were far out and not likely, blaming it on the Japanese (*Southern Illinoisan*, 4/30/95). The Michigan Militia claims 12,000 members in various counties. The Michigan Militia has fifteen phone lines, four computers, several faxes, a professional printing press and full television production capabilities (Smolowe, 1995).

Gary Krause, Police Chief in Fowlerville, Michigan, told of how one of his officers stopped a car in September 1994 and the three men inside had several weapons and much ammunition. They said they were Mark Koernke's bodyguards and had just completed maneuvers. They were charged but did not show for their arraignment six days later. Dozens of militia members did show up and taunted the police officers present (Smolowe, 1995). Mark Koernke became a nationwide celebrity after the Oklahoma City bombing. He has acted as a shortwave-radio personality, inspiring all over the country. Koernke distributes a two hour video called "America in Peril: A Call to Arms," giving ominous evidence of the one world conspiracy (Smolowe, 1995). Koernke discusses various violent acts to rid our government of its foes within, from using nylon rope to hang legislators (Lacayo, 1995) to pouring boiling water on the law enforcement agents who come to arrest you.

Mark Koernke came to the attention of mainstream America when it was rumored that he was wanted for questioning in connection with the Oklahoma City bombing. This story proved to be false. Koernke has given speeches in forty-four states and was an early figure in the militia segment of the right wing movement. Koernke reportedly had from his teenage years exhibited a fascination with guerilla type warfare and weaponry, had an intense dislike of authority figures, and much grandiosity, with attraction to the idea of martyrdom, and the ability to talk most people to death. He complained openly about "niggers and Jews" and big government. Koernke has served as a traveling salesman for the militia movement (Van Biema, 1995).

Timothy McVeigh reportedly had ties to the Michigan Militia who admitted he might have gone to a couple of meetings, but disclaimed any other ties. Both Terry Lynn Nichols, who was arrested after McVeigh and his brother James Douglas Nichols, who faced other charges, attended militia meetings. The Nichols were kicked out of the meetings for advocating violence (Woolf, April 30, 1995, 11a).

When questioned about the bombing, Tim McVeigh initially gave only his name, rank, and date of birth. As it happens, this is in the instructions for Prisoners of War in a manual published by the Michigan Militia (Gleick, May 8, 1995).

MILITARY INVOLVEMENT?
There are many questions about McVeigh's military training and whether this training and his connections to others in the

military aided him in the bombing incident. There have been previous incidents where those with military ties also had right wing ties. In 1986, three Marines from North Carolina's Camp Lejuene were ousted from the military for membership in a white supremacist group and one Marine testified he supplied the White Patriot Party with explosives and weapons. In 1992, a Green Beret sergeant pled guilty to stockpiling weapons and explosives and funneling them to white supremacist groups, including the KKK (Gleick, May 8, 1995).

Militias appear to get firepower from military stores. Supply clerk Mark Carter with the Michigan National Guard was caught peddling stolen military weapons and testified before a Congressional panel in November 1993 that physical security at military bases was a joke. Pentagon officials admit they are troubled with the existence of two underground newsletters circulated at military bases, the *Resister* and the *Groundhog*, which espouse some of the same anti-government beliefs as the controversial militia linked to McVeigh and the Nichols brothers. Investigators believe the fertilizer bomb in Oklahoma City was set off with non-electric igniters and blasting caps used in military demolition work (Gleick, May 8, 1995).

MILITIA BELIEFS

The Oklahoma City bombing caused a backlash against the militia movement, but also brought it publicity that helped it gets its message out and recruit new members. Before the bombing, gun shows had been a meeting place and information exchange for the growing militia movement, especially in Missouri, but after the bombing, members kept a low profile. Ray Sheil, public information officer for the 51st Missouri Militia, believes that the bombing adversely affected the militias. The 51st is named for the assault by federal officers on the Branch Davidian compound in Waco, Texas and the 51-day siege that ended in the deaths of eighty-five people, included several children. The militia movement has pointed to the Waco incident as proof that the federal government is violating Constitutional rights (Holleman, 1995).

There have been those in the militia movement that have accused the U. S. government or the United Nations of being responsible for the bombing in order to blame the militia movement. Pam Beesley operates an information service called "Gate Keepers" from Kansas City, Missouri. She contacted various media outlets to link allegations of the bombing to the possibility of a United Nations plot, saying that the United Nations, to overthrow a country, produces unrest in the country first (Bayles and Foster, 1995).

MILITIA OF MONTANA

Militias are energized to states' rights issues due to threats to the Second Amendment and their rights to gun ownership. However, they have also pushed anti-government thinking in a direction, that if followed to its logical conclusion, leads to one end: armed uprising. The most belligerent militia is the Militia of Montana with headquarters in the Cabinet Mountains near Noxon. An unidentified member told BBC last year, "This is probably where the war is going to begin, right here in Montana. We've got a lot more bullets than they do." John Trochmann, cofounder of the Montana group, along with his brother David and nephew Randy, distribute literature that would terrify many, such as photos of Soviet keeps said to be on American soil. He indicates that Russian troops are going to arrive in the U. S. as part of an international police force in his newsletter, *Taking Aim* (Weiss, 1995).

The Militia of Montana is a clearinghouse for anti-government, paramilitary and survivalist books and videotapes. After the Oklahoma City bombing, the group said that their phone and fax has been continually busy. They also send out "defensive tactics" handbooks including information on booby traps, claymore mines, and shooting down helicopters (*Southern Illinoisan*, 6/11/95a).

OTHER MILITIAS

Militias operate in more than half the states of the United States. Some of the militias merely promote the idea of an unorganized militia as suggested by the founders of our country. Other militia groups have their own agendas, beliefs, and have been more militant about suggested actions against the federal government.

Senate Subcommittee hearings on Terrorism, Technology, and Government Information, chaired by Sen. Arlen Specter, R-Pa., were held in June 1995. Norman Olson of the Michigan Militia and John Trochmann of the Militia of Montana were present, among others, claiming that high taxes, gun regulations and international agreements are the signs of impending dictatorship, with our government as the threat. Sen. Arlen Specter indicated that some militia officials have gone on record advocating the trial and hanging of public officials for treason and condoning the bombing in Oklahoma City. Specter cited studies showing the existence of at least two hundred and twenty-four militias, forty-five of which had ties to neo-Nazi and other white supremacist groups. Thirty-nine states had some form of militias, according to the studies (*Southern Illinoisan*, 6/16/95).

ARIZONA

David Espy   attempted to organize militias in Arizona beginning in 1994, with such names as the **Association of the Sons of Liberty and the Volunteer Militia.** He held meetings with the stated purpose of developing plans of action against the federal government which was passing legislation that infringed on private property and the Bill of Rights. Gary D. Hunt is also active in Arizona, and he is obsessed with the Branch Davidian incident in Waco, Texas. He passed out fliers in June 1994 applauding the effectiveness of in the Revolutionary War and advising of the need for them now. He appeared to plan a march in August 1994 by a handwritten note on the bottom of the flyer, but that never materialized. He labeled his flier, **Sons of Liberty No. 3** (Suall, et al, 1994).

Police Against the New World Order, led by Jack McLamb, a retired Phoenix police officer, discusses constitutional issues for lawmen *(Time,* May 8, 1995, 62-63). Police Against the New World Order (PANWO) is discussed in a later section involving violent acts.

COLORADO

Stewart Webb leads the **Guardians of American Liberties,** which is a multi-state organization centered in Boulder, Colorado.

He uses right wing radio shows to discuss conspiracy theories. There is a variety of patriot groups in Colorado and they support the militias springing up there. Many of the militias in Colorado call themselves **Patriots** and they promote the view that the federal government has betrayed its citizenry in such areas as abortion, taxation, freedom of speech and gun control. They urge people to form militias and stockpile weapons and other survival supplies (Suall, et al, 1994).

FLORIDA

Robert Pummer of the **Florida State Militia** in Stuart, Florida, urges members to buy ammo now as they will not be able to later (*Time*, May 8, 1995, 62-63). Pummer rouses his members with the same issues discussed by militias all over the country: gun control, David Koresh, Randy Weaver, Russian troops on U. S. soil, and other conspiracies. In the handbook for the Florida State Militia is a reading list of such publications as the Liberty Lobby's *Spotlight*, Edward Field's *The Truth at Last*, and other periodicals with racist and anti-Semitic themes. The **United States Militia** or alternatively **the 1st Regiment Florida State Militia** is based in Key Largo, Florida. It distributes material at conferences and has lists of regulations for its members and literature detailing complaints about the government. It says that militia units cannot be used against the police or governmental authority in Florida but makes an exception when such an entity commits crimes of violating their oaths of office or of the Constitution of Florida or the United States (Suall, et al, 1994).

IDAHO

Sam Sherwood of Blackfoot, Idaho, shepherds the **United States Militia Association,** headquartered there and supports Randy Weaver (*Time*, May 8, 1995, 62-63). He has recruited hundreds of militia members in at least a dozen of Idaho's forty-four counties. He has met opposition from law enforcement officials there (Suall, et al, 1994).

Sherwood holds monthly meetings in Twin Falls, Idaho, of one of the country's largest militias, claiming five thousand members in eleven states. Sherwood is a freelance computer consultant who wears army surplus garb and calls himself a reasonable militiaman. He says his group does not tramp around the hills with guns and plot against the government, but is, rather, a political association, seeking to preserve individual liberties, particularly the right to own guns (*Southern Illinoisan*, "Messenger of...," 6-11-95).

Bo Gritz, the Populist Party candidate and much decorated U. S. veteran, has an armed community of thirty families in Kamiah, Idaho, called **Almost Heaven** (*Time*, May 8, 1995, 62-63). In an interview with *Time* magazine's San Francisco bureau chief David S. Jackson, Gritz indicated that his followers were building a constitutional-covenant community near Kamiah, with the only requirement that one be willing to stand up for their neighbor's constitutional rights, with no conditions on race, color, creed, sexual preference, or anything of the like. He denied anyone having guns to his knowledge. Col. Gritz indicated that when the government is held accountable for what it does wrong, the American people will see that and unorganized militias will go back to what they were ten years before, the guy with a service rifle in his closet (Jackson, 1995).

INDIANA

Linda Thompson, an Indianapolis attorney, leads **American Justice Federation**. She says her goal is to stop the New World Order and get the truth out to the American public. She is an influential and controversial figure in the militia movement (*Time*, May 8, 1995, 62-63).

OTHER SMALL GROUPS

Edward Brown leads a small well organized group in New Hampshire, the **Constitution Defense Militia,** as New Hampshire law provides for an unorganized militia. This group opposes gun control laws and a large federal government.

Albert Esposito of the Monroe, North Carolina, **Citizens for the Reinstatement of Constitutional Government,** uses a similar vein in urging members to amass the 4 B's: Bibles, bullets, beans, and bandages.

Jon Roland leads the **Texas Constitutional Militia,** which had its first muster on April 19, 1994, with an E-mail network serving as an information highway for the underground. He claims to have penetrated government electronic intelligence.

James Roy Mullins, of the **Blue Ridge Hunt Club** in Virginia, was arrested for possessing a short barreled rifle and unregistered silencer in July 1994. Officials said that Mullins started the group to have members arm for war against the government.

Militias have now been identified in from twenty-seven states to thirty-nine states, depending upon who is identifying them. Some militias try to weed out racists and even have minority members, such as the **Hillsborough County Dragoons** of New Hampshire. The leader, Fitzhugh MacCrae, indicates that they have various minorities represented and favor good deeds for seniors, but believe in supporting the Second Amendment (*Time,* May 8, 1995, 62-63).

Militia groups operate in several other states, including Missouri, Ohio, and California. General Ray Looker recently participated in a panel discussion with Jerry Dale, former Poca-hontas County, West Virginia, Sheriff, a representative from the American Civil Liberties Union (ACLU), and others involving the right wing militias. Dale appointed himself the local monitor for the National Alliance when the group moved to his area in the mid 1980's. Looker is involved with militias in West Virginia, Ohio, Pennsylvania, Maryland, and Virginia. This panel discus-sion is to be aired over the Fox network in 1995 (Dale, 9/25/95).

Women are active in some militias. Joy Andrews of the **Placer County Unit of the California Unorganized Militia,** was featured in *USA Today* (5-16-95, 6D), as having the job of verifying rumors or finding them false, such as the fact that colored stickers on the back of county signs were not part of a conspiracy but rather maintenance tags of when the signs were last inspected. The **51st Missouri Militia** is named for the 51-day siege at Waco, Texas.

The most recent militia news story is still unresolved, but is being hotly debated. Michael Hill, a member of the Ohio militia, was shot and killed by local police outside Frazeyburg, Ohio, having been pulled over late at night for driving a car with homemade license plates bearing the word "militia." Authorities allege that he pulled a gun on the officer but militia witnesses say Hill was unarmed and was executed in cold blood (*Time*, 7/10/95).

STANDOFFS

The more militant of the militias and other extremist groups have created a policy problem for law enforcement officials. Because of criticism of federal officers after the Waco incident and Randy Weaver shootout and the Congressional hearing that followed, there are currently at least three fugitive cases in Montana alone where law enforcement is playing a cat and mouse game wit the fugitive, fearful of provoking another standoff and public scrutiny.

Calvin Greenup is the Montana coordinator for the **North American Volunteer Militia**, based in Indiana. Sheriff Jay Printz of Ravalli County, is trying to arrest Greenup without violence. Greenup is charged with a criminal conspiracy, allegedly plotting to kidnap local officials, try them in his own courts, and hang them. His son is wanted in connection with an assault on an officer and for jumping bail.

In another case, five fugitives, one wanted on federal tax evasion charges, are barricaded with assault rifles in a cabin now owned by the Internal Revenue Service. President Clinton has been asked for help but federal officials are treading with care. In a third incident, Gordon Selner is wanted for a shooting of a police officer more than a year ago. Authorities say they have not yet arrested him because they fear a confrontation will lead to a shootout (Post Dispatch, May 17, 1995; Koppel, May 22, 1995).

Daniel Levitas, who is involved in monitoring wing groups, was interviewed on ABC's "Night Line" on May 22, 1995, along with Ravalli County Sheriff Jay Printz. He estimated there are 50,000 Posse Comitatus members nationwide and the more extreme militias fit well with the Posse. He indicated that the current national frustration lends itself to more radical ideas. He believed that Greenup's supporters will be emboldened by a failure to go in and confront him, but if the police did go in, Greenup would become a martyr (Koppel, May 22, 1995).

Chip Berlet, who tracks right wing populism for the Political Research Associates in Cambridge, Massachusetts, explains the disgruntlement of working class people and farmers today, "You see the rise of a large group of disaffected middle-class and working-class people with a strong sense of grievance. None of the major parties speak for them." He warns the groups will be more militant if grievances are not resolved, that the militia message is the same whether shouted or whispered: We will be heard (Smolowe, 1995).

CHAPTER XI

Conspiratorial Activities Among Groups

L ooking at the history of right wing groups and how new groups have developed provides a basis for looking at the other factors in reference to the threat these groups pose to the U. S. government and targeted minorities. It is necessary to understand the historical context to understand the interconnections and some of their common goals.

The other factors to be examined can better be understood after having a knowledge of the historical roots of some of the groups. These factors include the conspiratorial nature of the groups, their pattern of escalating violence, the desire to establish a white American homeland, the theological basis for their beliefs, and their use of sophisticated communications, and paramilitary and survivalist training.

According to Suall and Lowe (1987) there has always been a certain amount of linkage among groups which promote bigotry, despite differences in their styles and their areas of emphasis. Suall and Lowe further stated that when the groups fall on hard times, such as having leaders arrested and other legal problems, one response is for groups of differing viewpoints to put aside their doctrinal differences and pull together for the themes that are common to the groups. In some cases, there may be dual memberships, such as Louis Beam being associated with the Texas Knights of the Ku Klux Klan and also being an Aryan Nations leader (ADL, 1988a).

However, these joint memberships are not the focus of the conspiracies being discussed. These conspiracies, instead, involve agreed upon activities among members of various right wing extremist groups.

THE ORDER

These linkages among groups continue to be evident, with representatives of various groups meeting together, planning together, and committing criminal acts together. The best example of these linkages was the Order, also called the Silent Brotherhood or Bruder Schweigen. The core membership came from two Identity groups, the Aryan Nations and the CSA. It included a neo-Nazi group, the National Alliance. It also included a number of Klansmen. In similar fashion, individuals charged by a federal grand jury in Fort Smith, Arkansas, included members of all three branches. Computer bulletin boards such as the Liberty Net have facilitated these connections (Suall and Lowe, 1987; ADL, 1985a).

Money from the Order's criminal acts was distributed to various right wing groups, according to grand jury testimony. This included $300,000 to Glenn Miller and the White Patriot Party which became the Southern National Front; $250,000 to Tom Metzger of the White Aryan Resistance (Martinez and Guinther, 1988); $50,000 to William Pierce of the National Alliance (ADL, 1988a; 1987a); $100,000 to Louis Beam of the Aryan Nations, formerly of the Texas Klan (Martinez and Guinther, 1988); and $10,000 to Dan Gayman, pastor of the Christian Identity church, Church of Israel (Flynn and Gerhardt, 1989).

While the FBI was able to uncover these expenditures, it was able to account for only about $600,000 of the money acquired by the Order during its crime spree. The remaining money may have been distributed to any of hundreds of Christian Identity, Klan, neo-Nazi, or Posse groups or could currently be in use financing further growth among right wing extremists (Coates, 1987).

Another indication of the scope of the right wing movement and its far reaching contacts is the fact that after members of the Order had fled the law, they were captured only after sympathizers from other groups attempted to hide them in Texas, New

Mexico, Georgia, the Carolinas, Virginia and Arkansas. Three members were eventually arrested at the CSA compound in Arkansas in a dramatic FBI assault in 1985, after attempts to shield them at that location (Coates, 1987).

Robert Miles "leaderless cells" theory could well have been used as the Order had plans for cells to break off and go underground to avoid detection and arrest.

ASSOCIATIONS BETWEEN GROUPS

The interconnections do not exist merely with the Order. In 1985, the Invisible Empire, Knights of the KKK, began an association with the Church of Jesus Christ-Christian, the Identity movement, and the Aryan Nations (Wade, 1987). Other Klan factions have also had connections with these groups, such as David Duke of the Knights of the KKK. Richard Butler, head of the Aryan Nations, established a compound at Hayden Lake, Idaho, with the idea of establishing a white separatist nation. He hosts Aryan Nations World Congresses attended by representatives of all the major right wing extremist groups.

The Aryan Nations World Congress in 1986 held at Hayden Lake, Idaho, had as its purpose the consolidation of these cooperating groups. They proposed to merge various movements, sects, and groups into a common white separatist movement (Scigliano, 1986). The 1983 Congress had been primarily involved in setting up Gordon Kahl as a martyr and setting the stage for cooperation among the various groups that later led to the Order.

Skinhead groups have been recruited by Christian Identity groups. Clark Martell's group, Chicago Area Skinheads (CASH), or Romantic Violence, attended meetings at Robert Miles' farm (ADL, 1988a; 1987d). Skinhead groups have also started forging alliances with the Ku Klux Klans. Skinheads had done more to popularize the far right movement than anything since the Order, until the more recent phenomenon of state militias came to national attention with the Oklahoma City bombing. Tom Metzger of the White Aryan Resistance has made particular efforts to utilize the skinhead movement as a tool of the right wing.

NATIONAL COMMODITIES AND BARTER EXCHANGE

Another very interesting and very novel example of the interconnections and conspiratorial system among the groups involves the concept of barter, a key Posse doctrine. It also involved efforts to avoid federal taxation and regulation. Movement leaders convinced supporters to convert their money to gold and silver to avoid paying income taxes. All wealth was then turned over to the National Commodities and Barter Association. The NCBA, in turn, paid all the necessary bills for the enrolled people.

The NCBA kept no paper receipts. The IRS raided five barter banks, seized ten tons of silver bullion, and estimated that the group laundered as much as half a million dollars each day for as many as 20,000 participants. A computer expert for the NCBA had rigged the computer which held the records with a "self destruct virus" which kicked in to erase all the files when government prosecutors tried to read the files to determine the identity of the participants (Coates, 1987). Assets were seized but the players were not identified.

This use of sophisticated computer technology is another indication of the level of expertise seen among the groups. Some sense of the scope of their activities can be seen from the estimated number of participants in the "bank" and the amount of money involved. This was only one of the efforts to thwart the IRS and federal reserve system. "Fractional reserve notes" discussed earlier are another way of protest and avoidance of using the United States currency system.

CHAPTER XII

Episodes of Violence

Although the Klans had a violent history and were responsible for the murders of thousands of black people (Ginzburg, 1988), their level of violence had declined by the 1960's. The 1960's showed violent activity by the Minutemen, but this violence had subsided, and less violent activity was seen until the last quarter of a century drew near. Some authorities on the extremist movement believe that the danger of violence rises, not when hopes and numbers are high, but when they shrink and an explosion results from the resulting frustrations (Scigliano, 1986). Several new hate groups began in the 1970's, possibly as a result of the frustrations seen in this country during that decade. These frustrations continued and new types of groups continued to form, such as the citizen militias in the 1990's.

In 1979, Roger Handley, Grand Dragon of Bill Wilkinson's Invisible Empire, Knights of the KKK, and others, were involved in a bloody confrontation involving the conviction of a retarded black man for raping a white woman (Wade, 1987). In 1981, UKA members hanged a black youth after being inspired by a cartoon of a black man hanging on a gallows in the Klan paper. This incident cost the Invisible Empire $7 million when a civil lawsuit was filed on behalf of the family of the deceased youth. In July 1983, Wilkinson's Klansmen firebombed the offices of Klanwatch at the Southern Poverty Law Center. Handley and other Klan leaders were charged with civil rights violations in May 1984 (Wade, 1987).

GORDON KAHL AND THE POSSE COMITATUS

The Posse Comitatus became more violent in the mid 1980's in the Midwest and far northwest. This trend may have been fueled by the plight of financially depressed farmers (Hoffman, 1986).

Gordon Wendell Kahl was a North Dakota farmer who was a zealous tax protestor and member of the Posse Comitatus. He killed two federal marshals near Medina, North Dakota on February 17, 1983, when these officers went to serve a warrant for probation violation. Kahl believed that the Internal Revenue Service was a collection agent for the Federal Reserve System, which, in turn, was a private corporation run by Jewish bankers. He had refused to pay taxes once and went to prison.

Kahl believed that if he ever went back to prison, he would be killed. Federal marshals were warned that he had stated he would not allow himself to be arrested and that he was well armed. These officers still attempted an arrest, an attempt which culminated in a shootout, at the cost of lost lives and crippling injuries, both to the officers and Gordon Kahl's compatriots. This was one of the earlier incidents when federal officers were criticized for the way in which they tried to carry out the arrest of a fugitive known to be armed and likely to fight. Gordon Kahl became a hero to many while he was on the run and was the subject of movies and much media attention. There was a great deal of popular support for Kahl with other Midwest farmers as well.

Kahl was not apprehended until four months later, in June 1983, in another shootout in which officers threw a tear gas canister which set off an inferno of exploding ammunition which, in effect, firebombed his hideout. He was killed, but not before he killed another local officer (Corcoran, 1990). It was Gordon Kahl who first brought the Posse Comitatus to national attention.

Gordon Kahl sets a pattern for the "dispossessed" individual discussed in the typology. He was a farmer, a working man, and his friends and compatriots were the same. He was the back-bone-of-America type who would not normally be seen as a criminal. Gordon Kahl believed in the doctrine of the Posse Comitatus and followed his beliefs to his death. Kahl and other individuals similar to him are very useful to the group spirit because they give the group respectability, someone to be a hero or a martyr, and to be acceptable to the average American citizen.

Events such as the Gordon Kahl episode and the accumulation and stockpiling of weapons perhaps set the stage for the Order to be created. Christian Identity has traditionally been involved in large accumulations of weapons. Before the Order began, two Identity members in California were arrested with what was then the largest cache of illegal weapons ever seized in this country, so large that it had to be photographed by an airplane to get all of it in one picture (Martinez and Guinther, 1988).

Gordon Kahl became a martyr for the right wing cause. The 1983 Aryan Nations World Congress was centered around talk of revenge for the killing of Gordon Kahl. The death of Gordon Kahl, perhaps more than any other single incident, began the trek of the extreme right down the path to criminal violence. The Order was borne shortly after the 1983 Aryan Nations Congress, the beginning of a new era of violence in the right wing.

The conspiracy begun at this 1983 meeting at Hayden Lake, Idaho, was a well funded, high tech guerilla war, including a plan to set up a nationwide computer system to link scattered right wing groups (*Time*, 1987a). Computers are widely used by the right wing movement to communicate in a media that has few government controls.

THE ORDER OR SILENT BROTHERHOOD
The Order was born in October 1983 and during its reign was responsible for three murders, including Jewish talk show host Alan Berg and a Missouri state trooper. It was also responsible for the most lucrative crime spree in U. S. history (Martinez and Guinther, 1988; ADL, 1985b). The Order robbed and plundered to raise funds for a revolutionary movement to establish a white American homeland.

Robert Mathews had plans to shut down a major U. S. city through terrorism in the months that followed his various actions (Flynn and Gerhardt, 1989). He had plans to blow up the

Boundary Dam and also to disrupt the electrical supply to the City of Los Angeles (Martinez and Guinther, 1988). The Order continued its activities for several months and their activities ranged from the counterfeiting enterprise that helped it begin, to the armored car heist, to murder, and cross country flight to avoid prosecution.

When federal officers raided the compound of Jim Ellison's group, the Covenant, the Sword, and the Arm of the Lord (CSA) on the Missouri-Arkansas border in April 1985 after the Order's demise, they found numerous deadly weapons and explosives and thirty gallons of poisonous cyanide. They also discovered an armory with the capability of making automatic weapons (Suall and Lowe, 1987; ADL, 1988a).

Despite the fall of the Order, Leonard Zeskind of the Center for Democratic Renewal, one of the watch dog groups who police the right wing extremists, stated that the broader Identity movement is doing very well. It is his contention that while more militant sects such as the KKK and Aryan Nations have lost power, more and more the groups consist of hard core zealots (Scigliano, 1986). Zealots, because of their belief system, may provide a more dangerous core of followers despite their smaller numbers. These zealots are the "dedicated followers" in the categorization provided in the typology.

The Order was reconstituted as the Bruder Schweigen Strike Force II. This group tried to take up where the Order left off by setting off four bombs in Coeur d'Alene, Idaho, in October 1986, to divert attention from a bank robbery that never took place. They also planned terrorist activities in shutting down utilities to major cities. They had earlier firebombed the residence of Father William Wassmuth who spoke out against the Aryan Nations (Howse, 1986; CDR, 1988). David Dorr, who succeeded Elden "Bud" Cutler as security chief for the Aryan Nations, was one of four Aryan Nations members arrested as part of the group (Martinez and Guinther, 1988; Suall and Lowe, 1987).

ARIZONA PATRIOTS

The midwest is known for anti-government, paramilitary activity (Best, 1995). In 1987, eight members of the Arizona

Patriots were convicted of conspiring to rob a Wells Fargo armored car in Nevada and using a car bomb to blow up an IRS complex in Ogden, Utah. Proceeds from the armored car robbery were going to be used to finance the construction of a survival camp for white supremacists in the desert outside Kingman, interestingly enough where Timothy McVeigh had been staying prior to the Oklahoma City bombing.

RANDY WEAVER AND THE RUBY RIDGE INCIDENT

Randy and Vicki Weaver and their three children had moved to Ruby Ridge, Idaho, believing in white separatism and various apocalyptic prophecies. On August 22, 1992, Randy Weaver, his wife, Vicki, his son, Sammy, and their friend, Kevin Harris began a siege that lasted eleven days. When it ended, Weaver's wife and son and a federal marshall were dead and Harris was wounded. Weaver was acquitted of killing the marshall in 1993 (Tharp, 1993). He was also acquitted on conspiracy charges in relation to the death. He did serve sixteen months on weapons charges (Lacayo, 8/28/95). As a disaster for the federal government in handling right wing groups, the Ruby Ridge incident ranks second only to the Branch Davidian assault in Waco, Texas, and by the time the final story is told, including Congressional hearings on the subject, it may reach the top slot.

The Weaver story started in 1989 when Weaver sold two illegal saw-off shotguns to an undercover informant and was later arrested. A clerk's error caused a court summons listing the wrong date in February 1991 for him to appear before a judge. When he did not appear on the correct date, an arrest warrant was issued. Weaver believed that the government would seize his property and family and in the months that followed, he sent messages threatening to shoot whoever would arrest him (Lacayo, 8/28/95). For eighteen months, federal agents had tried to arrest him in a non-violent manner.

U. S. marshals approaching the cabin on the mountain on August 21, 1992, started the family dog barking. Randy Weaver, Sammy, his fourteen-year-old son, and family friend, Kevin Harris, came outside, all being armed. A marshall shot the dog and Sammy fired in the marshall's direction, and then turned and ran. Sammy was killed by a gunshot to the back in the ensuing gunfight, and Marshall William Degan was killed by a gunshot to the chest. The marshals sent word they were pinned down by gunfire and the FBI's 50-member hostage-rescue team came in.

The day after the first shooting, an FBI sniper fired two rounds toward the residence. One shot wounded Weaver and the other killed Vicki and seriously wounded Harris. Vicki Weaver was standing behind an open cabin door when a shot from an FBI sniper went through the upper part of the door, killing Mrs. Weaver with a bullet to the head. She was holding her infant daughter, Elisheba, when she was killed.

The hostage-rescue team's original picture of Weaver, as given by the marshals, was a one-man commando squad. New rules of engagement were drawn up to say that armed adults "could be" shot on sight. Someone this later became "should be" but no one is taking the blame as to how this happened and the investigation is continuing (Lacayo, 8/28/95).

Former Special Forces hero Bo Gritz negotiated an end to the eleven day standoff. One major question appears to be whether or not law enforcement officers brought on violence that could have been avoided, and whether the officers had the right to fire on Weaver's wife. Vicki Weaver had written a 1991 letter to the Boise U. S. Attorney's Office stating "a long forgotten wind is beginning to blow. Do you hear the approaching thunder?" (Tharp, 1993). Perhaps Vicki Weaver only foretold the beginning of the thunder.

The Weaver incident and the current standoffs where federal officials are attempting arrests of well armed and politically difficult fugitives has forced federal law enforcement agencies to regroup and think about what is occurring. People are breaking the law, not paying taxes, possessing illegal guns, and doing other things in ways of protest against the government. Taking action against them, however, may only add fuel to the fire, as it has done in several cases already. It is a touchy area and there is no consistent policy on handling such situations, either locally or on the federal level.

The Weaver incident continued long after Randy Weaver was found not guilty of Marshall Degan's death. Gerry Spence, a sagebrush attorney and best-selling author, won a $3.1 million settlement from the government for Weaver and his three surviving daughters. The settlement kept the family from having to relive memories of their 11-day-old dead mother on the cabin floor and Sammy dead out in the woodshed. It also kept the government from facing an Idaho jury that might have awarded much more to the family, as well as having to to through a great deal of harrying testimony that would be well publicized (Lacayo, 8/28/95).

Various FBI officials have been disciplined and even suspended. There have been allegations of coverups and Senate hearings and a Justice Department investigation are being held on the Ruby Ridge incident.

Chris Fury, on ABC's Nightline (September 5, 1995), talked with Randy Weaver about the Ruby Ridge incident. Weaver described how his wife had held the door open to the cabin when Weaver, his daughter, and Kevin Harris were fleeing inside after having been shot at, and in Weaver's case wounded, by snipers. Weaver described how a shot went through the cabin door, went through Vicki's head and then bullet fragments and pieces of Vicki's bones went into Harris. Weaver also talked of allegations of shredded documents by FBI officials trying to cover up what happened at Ruby Ridge and who was responsible.

Testimony presented before the Senate panel investigating the Ruby Ridge incident found very different stories from Randy Weaver and the federal agents who had been involved. Randy Weaver testified in September 1995 before that panel and blasted law enforcement officials for improper actions and said that neither his extremist views nor his mistakes justified federal agents killing his wife and son during the standoff. Weaver stated that he made the mistake of selling the shotguns and not showing up for court, but that did not cause the federal agents to violate their oaths of office. Weaver stated that his wife was not wanted for any crime, there were no warrants for her, but she was gunned down in the doorway of her own home. Weaver's most serious allegation is that Lon Horiuchi, the FBI sniper, intentionally shot his wife. Justice Department officials contend the shooting was ruled accidental by everyone who studied it (Yost, 1995).

Randy Weaver testified that he had been set up by a federal informant because the ATF needed someone to "snitch" on the activities of white supremacist groups. Weaver also testified that his failure to appear in court was based in part on a distrust of the government, enhanced by what he saw as entrapment on the weapons violations. Weaver insisted that the informant encouraged him over a three-year period to sell a sawed-off shotgun and he finally agreed because he needed the $450 to buy groceries. Federal authorities, including ATF's Herb Byerly, the agent in charge of the operation, denied that the agency instigated the fatal events at Ruby Ridge or that they improperly targeted Weaver for gun charges (Meddis, 1995).

Weaver replied to questioning by Sen. Spencer Abraham during the Congressional hearing that at no time had any law enforcement officer arrived at his door, advised him of a warrant for his arrest, and attempted an arrest. Weaver stated that if he had been served with a warrant, he would have surrendered. He later again confirmed to Sen. Diane Feinstein that he would have gone peacefully, that he could not believe that all this had gone on over two sawed-off shotguns. Weaver further stated that in reference to an alleged incident in March 1992 when Sen. Feinstein asked if marshalls had come onto his property, he stated that strange people had come onto his property from time to time, but never identified themselves as federal agents. He said he had even had people come to his house for coffee that he suspected were federal agents, but they never identified themselves as such (C-Span, 1995).

The Ruby Ridge incident raises many questions about the actions of federal law enforcement officials. Randy Weaver did wrong and should have taken his punishment. However, even though he did not appear for court on a weapons charge, it appears highly unusual that he should have faced such organized and lengthy government surveillance. It appears from the Senate hearings that he may have been targeted because the government needed a snitch on Aryan Nations activities and kept working on Weaver, even to the point of being accused of entrapping him, for that reason.

Whatever the reason, the family was being kept under surveillance. When the federal marshalls were discovered by the male members of the group, Sam Weaver's dog was shot. This might not sound like so horrendous a crime, based on the theories of military engagement. However, seen from a more human viewpoint, it seems reasonable to assume that a fourteen-year-old, raised with weapons and armed, would be likely to fire his weapon when his dog was killed, with the only provocation being that the dog barked at intruders, who, Weaver alleges, did not identify themselves.

During Congressional hearings, Weaver testified that the girls had said that "Striker" (the dog) was acting weird. They went out to find the dog more worked up than they had ever seen them. Weaver said that was when he made the biggest mistake he ever made. He said he assumed the dog was after large game, such as a bear or cougar and sent Sam and Kevin Harris one way after the dog and he went the other way to flush out the animal. He had to go down a logging road and Cooper or Rodrick (federal agents) jumped out and yelled at him. He ran back and yelled for Sam and Kevin. He then heard a shot and heard the dog yelp. He said that he yelled for Sam and Kevin to go home as someone had shot the dog. He said that Sam fired two shots in anger and then Weaver fired a .12 gauge shotgun in the air to draw attention to himself and away from Sam. He jammed the shotgun and fired three more shots with another gun and yelled for Sam who yelled he was coming. There were more shots and Kevin Harris came to him to tell him that Sam had been killed. The family was distraught.

Regardless of who was to blame for the gunfire that occurred at this point and left Sam Weaver and U. S. Marshall William Degan dead, things might still have been deescalated before the further bloodshed. However, it was after this that the questionable and probably unconstitutional order was given that allowed snipers the discretion that they "could" or "should" shoot armed adults on sight.

Weaver had retrieved Sam's body, cleaned him up and put him in the shed outside the house. The next day he was outside to check on Sam's body, put his gun in his other hand to open the shed door and was shot in the back by a sniper. He said his daughter, Sarah, was also outside and pushed him toward the house. His wife had come out after hearing the shot and was holding the door open for him, Sarah, and Kevin Harris. There was another shot as they went through the door and Kevin sprawled to the floor. Vicki fell to the floor, with a gunshot to the head, with the baby under her. The baby was all right, but bloody (C-Span, 1995).

Randy Weaver was wounded when he was not firing on anyone, with the justification given that because there was a helicopter overhead, he might have fired on it, since he was armed. Then, his wife was killed as the trio fled inside. Congressional hearings have addressed the contention that the FBI's psychological experts were concerned that Vicki Weaver might kill the children rather than surrender. Weaver contends that she was purposely killed for this reason.

Sam Donaldson interviewed Randy Weaver on *Nightline* on nationwide television on September 6, 1995. Weaver stated that after his wife had been killed and Harris wounded, four hundred law enforcement people with armored cars surrounded his home on the mountainside. He said that at no point had anyone asked him to turn himself in until Bo Gritz came to ask him to turn himself in. He said that Col. Gritz later advised his attorney that he had been given a deadline of August 30 for Weaver to give up or further action would be taken to end the standoff. Weaver alleges that Gritz was told by FBI Agent Rogers that Vicki Weaver was targeted by sniper Lon Horiuchi because she was the maternal head of the household and might kill the children (Donaldson, 1995).

All the facts may never be known. With the available facts, however, the Ruby Ridge incident is pointed to as a complete fiasco by a federal law enforcement agency and with allegations that that agency tried to cover-up rather than take responsibility for their mistakes.

ANTI-ABORTION PROTESTS AND VIOLENCE
White supremacists leaders have jumped on the anti-abortion bandwagon as a new rallying point for their own revolution,

although some of the more traditional anti-abortion leaders have not claimed them. The American Front, a skinhead group has joined Operation Rescue protestors at Oregon clinics and the Ku Klux Klan has also been involved. John Burt, regional director of the anti-abortion group, Operation Rescue, was a former Florida klansmen, and has been closely involved with people accused of killing abortion doctors, even Paul Hill, who has now been convicted. Michael Griffin, the man who murdered Dr. David Gunn in Pennsacola, Florida in 1993, was a volunteer at a home for unwed mothers operated by Burt. The Ku Klux Klan has been putting out "wanted" posters on abortion doctors and believes that abortion is another tool of the Jews to destroy the white race (Ross, 1994). More and more right wing extremist groups are joining other Christian groups in abortion protests and advocating violence.

BLUE RIDGE HUNT CLUB AND MINNESOTA PATRIOTS
In 1994, federal agents raided the home of the man who started the Blue Ridge Hunt Club, James Roy Mullins. They recovered illegal guns and silencers. They also found documents advocating guerilla warfare, assassination and attacks on bridges and airports, all in the name of gun control protest. The leader and a member await sentencing after pleading guilty to a federal weapons charge.

In February 1995, two members of the anti-tax Minnesota Patriots Council were convicted on federal terrorism charges. They plotted to use chemical poisons against unnamed human targets ("America. . .", 1995)

THE OKLAHOMA CITY BOMBING
Until April 19, 1995, in Oklahoma City, the 1927 dynamite explosion at a school in Bath, Michigan, on May 19, was the worst mass attack against a community in U. S. history. Thirty-eight children and seven adults were killed by a demented farmer, a madman angry at higher taxes and consolidated school systems (McGuire, 1995).

The world ended on April 19, 1995, for one hundred sixty-nine victims of the Alfred P. Murrah Federal Building bombing in

Oklahoma City. Some experts believe that the bombing was patterned after *The Turner Diaries*, which details a fictional account of a car bombing of an FBI headquarters. The bombing in the book took place at 9:15am, nearly the time of the Oklahoma City bombing, and used ammonium nitrate fertilizer, the same as the Oklahoma City bombing.

The Turner Diaries had previously been used as a blueprint by Robert Mathews and the Order and their efforts to overthrow the federal government. William Pierce AKA Andrew Macdonald, the author of *The Turner Diaries*, states he has sold 200,000 copies in seven printings. He said "I've not the faintest idea whether people arrested or others who might have been involved in the Oklahoma City bombing have even heard of the book (Post Dispatch, 4/24/95, 5b).

Victims of the federal building bombing included several federal agencies, including DEA, Customs, the Secret Service, and various other service departments. It also included America's Kids Day Care Center, where fifteen children died in the bombing (*USA Today*, 5-12-95).

Even as the Alfred P. Murrah Building was being bombed, a ceremony was being held in Waco, Texas, by Branch Davidians and the North Texas Militia to commemorate the Waco incident. Tim McVeigh, who became the chief suspect in the Oklahoma City bombing, had earlier made a pilgrimage to the site. The Waco seige has been a rallying point for militias and others in the right wing extremist movement. A cottage industry developed in videos about Waco, with such videos as "Waco: The Big Lie" and "Waco II: The Big Lie Continues." Waco was the spark and a factor in bringing militias together (Koppel, 5/5/95).

From early on, Tim McVeigh and two brothers, James and Terry Lynn Nichols, were at the forefront of those believed responsible for the bombing. Investigators focused much of their attention on Kingman, Arizona, where McVeigh had lived for five months in 1994 with a pregnant girlfriend. During that time, a small bomb exploded in a residential area, damaging some windows of some houses but causing no injuries. Areas around Kingman have been used for explosives training by the Arizona Patriots, a right wing group that denounces the federal government in radio shows and tapes. McVeigh had checked into a Kansas motel on April 14, giving his own name but James Nichols' Decker, Michigan, address. At least three witnesses say McVeigh was outside the federal building in Oklahoma City on the morning of the bombing. An hour and twenty minutes after the bombing, McVeigh was pulled over for driving with no license plates by state trooper Charles Hanger in Perry, Oklahoma, sixty miles from Oklahoma City. The trooper saw a shoulder harness containing a Glock semiautomatic pistol. McVeigh was jailed on these charges. Shortly before he was to go to court two days later and possibly be released on $500 bail, the FBI contacted the local state's attorney and told them to hang onto their prisoner (Duffy, 1995; Gleick, 5/1/95). Why Timothy McVeigh was so careless in his choice of getaway cars and why he offered no resistance may never be known. On the other hand, if he did have a political agenda involving his role in the bombing, he may have assumed the role of martyr in order to have his "day in court" to espouse his beliefs.

McVeigh was familiar with the Nichols brothers, having lived for a time with James Nichols in Decker. Neighbors there said that McVeigh dealt in guns. McVeigh and possibly Terry Nichols attended meetings of the Michigan Militia, but that group denied them being members (Gleick, 5/1/95).

McVeigh and the Nichols brothers had been making bombs as early as 1992 with brake fluid, gasoline, and diesel fuel at the Michigan farm, according to the FBI. James Nichols told the FBI that the three of them had made "bottle bombs," and admitted that he had made other explosive devices. Books about bomb making with ammonium nitrate were found with his brother's possessions. The FBI found twenty-eight fifty-pound bags of ammonium-nitrate fertilizer, fuel oil, blasting caps, large quantities of hydrogen peroxide, aluminum powder and large fuel tanks, all of which can be used to make bombs, according to the FBI's affidavit (Poor, 1995).

Tim McVeigh became a puzzle of contradictions. He was seen as someone who would succeed, but was not much of a student. He was a straight arrow soldier, but remained mostly a loner in the Gulf War infantry unit where he was assigned. McVeigh had recently been involved with tax protestor groups and anti-government types, believing that the Army implanted a computer chip in his buttocks. He was angry over the Branch Davidian incident in Waco, Texas, and he went everywhere armed.

The Oklahoma City bombing indictments were handed down in August 1995 and the indictments contained only an outline of how the bombers allegedly blew up the Alfred P. Murrah Federal Building on April 19, 1995. George J. Church, writing for *Time* magazine (1995) indicated that the sparseness of the indictments indicates the alleged conspiracy was a small-time affair in everything except the results. Michael Fortier was the only alleged helper named, in that he helped McVeigh case the Murrah building. Fortier pleaded guilty to a separate indictment charging him with transporting stolen property (guns sold to raise money for explosives) and with perjury. He is to testify against Timothy McVeigh and Terry Nichols who have been charged by the federal grand jury with the bombing.

Church goes on to describe an interview with Jennifer Mc-Veigh in which she describes FBI tactics of playing mind games with her, putting her and her mother in a room with huge posters with Jennifer's name and a picture all blown up with possible charges against her like life imprisonment. She said they took books, including library books she should have returned, that she was using to write a paper, and her word processor, which still has not been returned because they needed it to run a tape they got from her. Church questions what crimes the government was going to seek indictments for against her. She reportedly told the government about a couple of incidents with McVeigh, but the worst she could be charged with would be knowing about a crime and not reporting it (this being him driving around with explosives and another time committing a robbery). If she had been threatened with the death penalty, it appears to have been a bluff.

The defendants in the Oklahoma City bombing case are awaiting trial at the publication of this book. Whether or not they are solely responsible for the bombing that took so many lives is not a question that can be answered at this time.

THE BOMB CULTURE

The rise in violence is seen by some as an aftereffect of the culture that makes information available on how to make bombs and create other havoc upon whomever the reader wants to attack. An increase in bombings is seen as perhaps coming from the wide dissemination of bomb know-how that has become an industry in the United States.

In the past few decades, there has been a great rise in mail order publishing companies whose most popular products are "burn and blow" books that describe in detail how to make land mines, booby traps, and bombs. The information is also available through Internet computer bulletin boards. The most notorious publisher is *Palidin Press* of Boulder, Colorado, founded by two Special Forces veterans of Vietnam. They have forty books and videos on making explosives. One book is *Homemade C-4: A Recipe for Survival,* billed as being used "when something more powerful than commercial dynamite is needed," with the caveat that it is "for informational purposes only" (Farley, 1995, p. 56).

AND THAT'S NOT ALL. . .

In the wake of the Oklahoma City bombing, strange criminal acts were reported as possible follow-up acts. In the southwestern part of Illinois, in a little town called Dupo, **seven hundred** pounds of ammonium nitrate fertilizer were stolen, already mixed with diesel fuel. These were taken from a stone quarry, stored there to be used as explosives in the quarry. The stolen materials have not surfaced and no one has claimed responsibility for the theft.

An even stranger move was reported by Larry W. Harris, a white supremacist sympathizer with the militia movement, a member of the National Alliance and with ties to the Aryan Nations. He was arrested for buying bubonic plague virus through the mail. This was a freeze dried bacteria, harmless in that form, but reconstitutable. No one knows what he intended to do with it (Post Dispatch, 5/17/95). The easy access to weapons of mass destruction and proliferation of written materials and computer programs for bomb making, weapons, and survivalism has made it possible for any variety of nuts to wreak havoc upon an unsuspecting American public.

OPERATION VAMPIRE KILLER 2000

Some publications only hint that violence **may** be needed. Operation Vampire Killer 2000 (1992) outlines a plan for police and national guardsmen to combine to stop the development of theNew World Order by the year 2000. This movement, Police Against the New World Order, is led by Jack McLamb, a retired Phoenix police officer. It encourages not assisting IRS agents because they are an essential part of the New Order plan to rob Americans of their wealth. The New World Order is seen as working toward martial law, race wars, and perpetuating a fraud of imminent world collapse and a threat of UFO's.

The plan to disarm the public is discussed. The booklet details how some good citizens will give up their guns when asked and then officers will have to decide if they will kill their countrymen who will not give up their guns. The publication believes that the plan depends upon police officers for their assistance and encourages them to prevent the New World Order from taking hold, without specifically suggesting a call to **violent** action.

The publication states that it is detailing the plan of the Internationalists, but the primary goal of the special police publication is to "promote an active program that will defend America from those at work forming an oligarchy of Imperialism against this nation of free people." The publication urges that it be passed out to every Police Officer and National Guardsman that the person who possesses it knows.

Operation Vampire Killer 2000 states that one should seek out those who are said to be enemies of the government, the right wing fanatics and radicals because they are great American Patriots and are listed as Public Enemy Number One because they are the only people in the nation fighting the New World Order. The publication states that these so called "crazy" Americans meet to non-violently plan to save our nation and they are the working class, the spirit of America. It goes further, however, to say that they will "go to war" against those who would try to enslave them.

While *Operation Vampire Killer 2000* does not specifically promote violent acts, it insinuates that such acts may be necessary. It encourages law enforcement and military personnel to take matters into their own hands as to what is correct and proper action.

SKINHEAD VIOLENCE

Skinhead violence is constantly in the news. It had become almost routine in the northwest by the late 1980's. Skinheads beat up people who looked gay, Jewish, or non-white. Of particular interest in discussing right wing extremists and their ties to skinheads was the murder of Mulugeta Seraw, an Ethiopian youth killed by skinheads in Oregon in November 1988 (Ridgeway, 1990). Prior to this murder, agents from the White Aryan Resistance (WAR) met with East Side White Pride, the skinhead group involved, and encouraged them to physically attack minorities. Because skinheads had been influenced by the White Aryan Resistance and their leaders, Tom and John Metzger, the Metzgers and the White Aryan Resistance were included in a civil suit under vicarious liability provisions (ADL,1990).

In 1993, suspects aligned with three white power right wing groups, Tom Metzger's White Aryan Resistance (WAR), the Church of the Creator in Florida, and the Fourth Reich Skinheads plotted to bomb the First African Methodist Episcopal Church in Los Angeles. They planned to kill the pastor and many of the congregation, then target other well known blacks across the country, such as sports stars and television stars. They believed this would trigger an all-out race war. The conspiracy was nipped in the bud before it was carried out (Monroe, 1993). Although the news article did not point it out, this is very similar to incidents mentioned in *Hunter,* Andrew Macdonald AKA William Pierce's sequel to *the Turner Diaries.* In *Hunter,* the main character, Oscar Yeager, a Defense Department contractor, strategically attacks blacks, biracial couples, and prominent Jews in an effort to start a race war, and force white Americans to take a stand.

Skinheads have murdered in every corner of the country. In 1990 in New York, Julio Rivera was fatally stabbed and beaten with a hammer by three men connected with Doc Martens Stompers because he was gay. Later in 1990 in Houston, two skinheads did a "boot party" with a fifteen-year-old Vietnamese immigrant named Hung Truong, stomping him to death. In Salem, Oregon, in September 1992, three American Front members firebombed the apartment of a black lesbian and gay white man, killing both. In Alabama, in early 1992, three skin-heads knifed a homeless black man, Benny Rembert, killing him in celebration of Hitler's birthday (VanBiema, 1993).

Pennsylvania saw even greater violence and mayhem, this time within a family. Bryan and David Freeman were the sons of Brenda and Dan Freeman, devoted parents who were members of the Jehovah's Witness sect. The Freemans were worried about their sons and the way they were acting, dressing, and treating others. After much conflict over their skinhead life style, the two boys killed their parents and their eleven-year-old brother. These boys who had emotional problems without the skinhead move-ment involvement, had become killers. David had "Sieg Heil," the Nazi salute, tattooed on his forehead and Bryan had "Ber-zerker" on his forehead, the skinhead term for someone who gets drunk and kills people, also a skinhead rock band, and maybe what the Freemans called the skinhead group they were trying to form (Miller and Stokes, 1995).

UNBALANCED INDIVIDUALS
WHO LEAN TO THE RIGHT

All across the landscape of the right wing, strange people have reacted to the talk of conspiracy, anti-Semitism, Armageddon, tax protest, gun control, and associated themes with disastrous results for those living about them. They have come up with their own version of Armageddon, spicing up the theology they learned from their mentors. Assistant U. S. Attorney Gene Wilson viewed these sporadic episodes of violence as a major danger, more so than the activities of organized groups such as the Order. People loosely connected to right wing extremist groups and loosely connected to reality are inspired by the writings and teachings to commit aberrant acts that they think support the cause and teachings.

While not in the mainstream of the right wing extremist movement, various individuals have been influenced by the movement and gone off on their own psychotic way to establish their version of a survivalist compound and/or commit acts against those whom they see as the enemy. While the people and groups who influence them may not acknowledge nor approve of their actions, it is impossible to deny their attachment to the right wing teachings, and there is no way to estimate how many people are affected (Coates, 1987).

These are the "delusional personalities" discussed in the typology. They are identified by their frail grasp of reality and the influence that right wing teachings and doctrine exert on their actions. It is this connection to the movement that separates them from other persons with ideas that may not have roots in reality. Following are brief accounts of some of the more bizarre adherents to the far right movement.

MICHAEL RYAN AND RULO, NEBRASKA

Michael Ryan met Jim Wickstrom of the Posse Comitatus in 1982 and was given the "Power of the Arm Test." He was told that those with the "Power" were able to get advice directly from God on matters from the trivial to the profound. This test involved holding up one's arm at a forty-five degree angle while the testor, who had the "Power," grabbed the wrist of that hand with one hand and the person's shoulder with the other. Actually the person holding the shoulder had complete control of whether or not the person being tested arm's stood up or fell down, so, in that manner, they truly did have the "Power" (Coates, 1987).

Ryan used the "Arm Test" for everything. He had been introduced to Posse doctrine in the early 1980's when he began reading and listening to taped sermons. Ryan started his own right wing survivalist compound in Rulo, Nebraska, where he practiced polygamy with the several women there. He forced other men to sodomize the compound's goat, and forced a father to have oral sex with his own child as a punishment. Ryan later murdered several members, including that child (Coates, 1987). Although Ryan and indeed some of the others to be mentioned, would be psychotic no matter where they were or who they listened to, significant aspects of far right beliefs and calls for action were involved in their activities.

DAVID LEE RICE AND THE DUCK CLUB

David Lewis Rice received messages from friends in outer space, feeding an obsession with Communists, the Federal Reserve, and Jewish international bankers (Prochnau, 1986). He had been attending meetings of the ultraconservative Duck Club Chapter in Seattle, Washington. He had been told by the President of the Seattle Duck Club that Charles Goldmark was "regional director of the Communist party." Rice had found himself a mission and a target. This was enough reason for Rice to stab and bludgeon the entire Goldmark family, holding the belief that they were Communists and Jews, although they were neither (Coates, 1987; Prochnau, 1986). While he was not involved in mainstream right wing functioning except for his Duck Club connections, the influence caused a psychotic personality to commit murder.

COKEVILLE, WYOMING

In 1986, David and Doris Young concocted a strange scheme to raise money to start an Aryan "new race." They held 167 people, mostly school children, captive at theCokeville, Wyoming, grade school, demanding millions in ranson. They planned to take half the children with them to an unidentified island to start their new race. The plan backfired when a gasoline bomb went off accidentally, burning Doris horribly, as well as many of thechildren. Young killed his wife and then himself (Coates, 1987).

DAVID KORESH AND THE BRANCH DAVIDIANS

David Koresh led a group of the Branch Davidian religious sect in Waco, Texas, and had convinced himself that he was to be the second coming of Christ. Koresh and the Branch Davidians have become a rallying point for gun control activists, religious activists, civil libertarians, and just about anyone who is anyone with a cause. Many of them seem to forget what was going on with members of the sect and what David Koresh was doing there. Regardless of whether or not the situation was botched when an attempt was made to raid the compound, maybe those supporting his memory should decide whether or not he was really hero material and remember some of the others who died there.

David Koresh was under investigation for ten months because of evidence that he was building a large stockpile of illegal weapons, including material to make live hand grenades, along with concerns that he might be abusing children and contemplating leading his followers in a mass suicide.

Agents of the Bureau of Alcohol, Tobacco, and Firearms (BATF) attempted a raid at theBranch Davidian compound. They found Koresh ready for armed battle and expecting them. Four federal agents and up to six cult members were dead and fifteen ATF agents and several cultists, including Koresh, were wounded. This began a 51-day siege and standoff of the FBI, with Koresh talking of doomsday and sometimes offering hope at times that when he reached the correct religious pinnacle he would give up (Rainie, 1995).

All during the siege, Koresh made it clear that he feared he would be raped if sent to prison, a fate often befalling child molesters. Although there had been no criminal accusations, widespread publicity said that he had sex with cult members as young as ten or twelve years old (Rankin, 1995). Koresh was the only man at the compound allowed to have sex with the females there, as only his seed was pure.

On April 19, 1993, the FBI assaulted the compound by ramming the wall to insert tear gas. Cultists who survived contend that the tank knocked over a lamp or somehow ignited a propane canister. FBI officials say aerial surveillance using infrared showed that there had been three separate fires breaking out within fifty seconds, indicating the cultists torched the compound (Rainie, 1995).

The FBI notified Koresh prior to the tear gas assault where the tear gas would be inserted in order that he could move the children away from that area (Gibbs, 1993). Sometime after the gas was inserted, the compound burst into flame. Seventy-five people died, including Koresh and more than twenty children.

The Waco siege is remembered for some questionable judgment on the part of the law enforcement agencies who stormed the compound. During the months prior to the attack, the agents had plenty of justification to enter the compound, including machine gun fire, pineapple type grenades delivered there and then black powder to make live grenades. When the raid did occur, affidavits have been filed to show that Koresh knew of the raid in advance and most of the adults in the compound were armed and ready. The ATF says that the Branch Davidians fired first and an attorney for the Branch Davidians blames the ATF for firing the first shot (Gibbs, 1993).

After the initial assault and four officers killed, everyone sat and waited fifty-one days and played mind games with Koresh, disregarding the advice of psychologists and even their own law enforcement siege and religious fanaticism experts. No one knew how to end the siege peacefully. When it did end, with a bang, federal agents were criticized again, along with Janet Reno, the Attorney General, for how it was handled.

Koresh let the federal agents know the depth of his maniacal ideas. The weekend of April 10, he sent the FBI two letters from God, stating, "I am your God and you will bow under my feet. do you think you have the power to stop my will?" (Gibbs, 1993, p. 35).

Koresh treated Branch Davidians in a manner typical of cult leaders. He rationed their food and took all the possessions of new members. He forced the men to be celibate and took their wives and daughters as concubines, as young as eleven. He played mind games and paddled the men, or made them lie down in raw sewage as punishment and did not allow them to bathe. Psychologists classified him as a psychopath, and described how these people can be charming, bright, and persuasive (Lacayo, 5/3/93).

Koresh's letters should give pause to anyone who sees him as a hero and a martyr. On April 10, he spoke further, "I offer to you my wisdom. I offer to you my sealed secrets. . . I AM your God and you will bow under my feet. . .I AM your life and your death. I AM the Spirit of the Prophets and the Author of their testimonies. . ."

On April 11, "My hand made heaven and earth, My hand also shall bring it to the end. . . Please listen and show mercy and learn of the marriage of the Lamb. Why will be you be lost?" (Signed) Yahweh Koresh (*Time*, 5/3/93, p. 36).

The Treasury Department's 500-page study of the Waco incident is known as the "Blue Book." This report details a continuing trail of errors that led to the disaster. For instance, in an undercover house established adjacent to the compound, the agents posed as college students, but were too old, carried expensive briefcases and drove nice cars. It was later learned that Koresh had run checks on the cars and found three of four had no outstanding credit liens. Raid planners chose a direct assault because they believed Koresh never left the compound, but he had done so several times, within weeks of the February raid. Faulty intelligence led agents to believe guns were kept in a central location when they were actually distributed throughout the compound for easy access. Also, ATF ended surveillance eleven days before the raid and tactical planners were unaware of that until the review team told them. These were only some of the more blatant errors and intelligence mistakes made (Larson, "How a Cascade of Errors. . .," 1995).

The David Koresh and Branch Davidian siege has not yet ended. Congressional hearings are being held about who was to blame, what was done wrong, and the fact that although the group's religious beliefs should not be cause for targeting it, neither should the beliefs allow the group to operate outside the law (Rankin, 1995).

Although the botched raid was begun by the ATF and it was the FBI who was in charge when the seige ended, the ATF has faced criticism after criticism to the point that over the years, they may be shying away from prosecutions of licensed gun dealers and going after more politically safe targets such as crack gangs, outlaw bikers, and ordinary killers. David Koresh had appeared to be an ideally safe target for the ATF, an apparent madman leading a cult armed with vast quantities of weapons. Waco appeared to be a place where the ATF could look good (Larson, "ATF Under Siege," 1995).

Dean M. Kelley, counselor for religious liberty at the National Council of Churches, criticized the FBI for fundamentally misunderstanding the Branch Davidians, portraying them as cold-blooded killers holding children hostage when they were really adults voluntarily and devotedly following a visionary they believed was touched by the finger of God. Alan A. Stone, professor of psychiatry and law at Harvard Law School was asked to join a federal review panel in summer 1993 to make recommendations regarding law enforcement reforms following Waco. He waited until he had researched the facts on his own to make a recommendation. His conclusion was that the Davidians had probably set the fire themselves in which they perished, but that bull-headed FBI pressure tactics probably drove them to it, just as the FBI's own psychological experts had warned it might (Rankin, 1995).

Stone's thirty-four-page analysis of the incident describes the miscalculation made by the FBI. "They tried to show him (Koresh) who was the boss. What went wrong at Waco was not that the FBI lacked expertise in behaviorial science or in the understanding of religious groups. Rather, the commander on the ground and others committed to traditional law enforcement practices disregarded those experts and tried to assert control and demonstrate to Koresh that they were in charge" (Rankin, 1995, 11A). Stone believes that Koresh chose mass suicide, rather than submission.

Hearings held in July 1995 produced sparks following party lines, with Republicans accusing federal agents of bungling the operation. Democrats accused Republicans of letting the National Rifle Association influence important parts of the committee investigation. A teenager also testified that sect leader Koresh had sexually molested her when she was ten years old (*Time*, 7/31/95, 18).

The North Texas Constitutional Militia held a memorial for those killed at the Branch Davidian compound at the same time the federal building in Oklahoma City was being bombed. Survivors of the Waco incident believe the government was working against its citizens. Clive Doyle, a survivor of the blaze and informal leader of the survivors, hold services every Saturday with some worshippers reportedly expecting to see Koresh resurrected (Bellafante, 1995).

WILLIAMSON COUNTY, ILLINOIS

Williamson County, Illinois, is located in the very southern part of the state, and is known locally as "Bloody Williamson" due to its history of labor unrest, murder of scab laborers, and murderous gangsters during the prohibition era.

The general election in Williamson County ended with a bang the night of November 8, 1994. James E. Johnson, who stated in a letter to U. S. Senator Paul Simon that he was a member of the Cherokee nation and had been labeled as a "personality disorder" by the Veterans Administration, allegedly fired shots from a semi-automatic weapon and a handgun at the Herrin Police Department, Marion Police Department, two Masonic lodges, and the Williamson County Courthouse, the last of which had people assembled to count the general election votes and watch the totals come in.

For several years, Johnson had been sending out letters to various government officials, complaining of a conspiracy of Freemasonry and Talmudic Jews to control local officials. Johnson distributed several pages of his complaints all over the county to various officials (Johnson, 1994), stating that he would take action in seven days if his grievances were not acted upon, which would have been Friday of election week. No one knows why he took the offensive on Tuesday. He is awaiting trial, presently being found unfit to stand trial, on various charges involving armed violence. He claimed no ties to other groups and none of them claimed him. He did address the group of people in Benton, Illinois, mentioned earlier in reference to patriot groups, shortly before the shooting.

CHAPTER XIII

White American Homeland

The desire to start a new Aryan race before the coming of Armageddon is a central doctrine to the far right wing extremist movement. It is shown even more graphically in studying the efforts of the various right wing groups to carve their own nation out of various parts of the United States, particularly in the Pacific northwest.

The central theme of many right wing extremist groups has been this plan to establish a white American homeland, free of blacks and Jews, generally to be in the Pacific northwest, although various groups want their own little piece of the world to be an all-white territory. Christian Identity believers have traditionally believed that the field of Armageddon will be in Nebraska or Kansas (Flynn and Gerhardt, 1989; ADL, 1983).

Most of the Aryan groups would like to secede from the Union, which they call the Zionist Occupation Government (ZOG), to form their own nation (King, 1986), with the capital being Hayden Lake, Idaho. The official plan in taking over the northwest is to breed enough Aryans so the kingdom will be theirs by default, but some extremists have not been able to wait and began armed revolt (Jordan, 1986).

NORDLAND

The Nationalist Socialist White People's Party, first called the American Nazi Party, now known as the New Order, is the oldest and most solid of the neo-Nazi groups. This group has relocated to New Berlin, Wisconsin, and seeks to establish a National Socialist Community called Nordland at that location (ADL, 1988a).

ISOLATION AND COMMUNICATION

William Pierce of the National Alliance moved his group to an isolated area also, but in the eastern part of the country. His group, and their associated Cosmotheist Church, are headquartered in Mill Point, West Virginia, in Pocahontas County. This is a mountainous, isolated area, with no towns of any size nearby and in an area honeycombed with limestone caverns.

Robert Miles, now deceased, and William Pierce have probably been the most intellectual minds of the right wing movement. Now, only Pierce remains as the "brains" of the movement and he remains in solitude on top of his mountain, operating a shortwave and AM radio program, publishing enterprise, and computer network from there.

NORTHWEST TERRITORIAL IMPERATIVE, THE 10% SOLUTION

Robert Miles operated the Mountain Church or Mountain Kirk, in Cohoctaw, Michigan. He was one of the thinkers of the movement (Flynn and Gerhardt, 1989; Suall and Lowe, 1987). He advocated a "10% Solution" which would mean setting aside the five states of the Pacific northwest for a White Aryan Republic. This "Northwest Territorial Imperative" was endorsed by the Knights of the KKK from Tuscumbia, and key activists moved to the area.

ARYAN NATIONS

Richard Butler established his Church of Jesus Christ-Christian and his Aryan Nations compound at Hayden Lake, Idaho. It has long been the plan of Butler and the Aryan Nations to make Idaho the home of an independent Aryan nation (Howse, 1986). Many right wing adherents relocated to the Pacific northwest to support that idea.

The Aryan Nations Conference, in July 1986, adopted a strategy calling for the creation of a separate white republic in the five states of the Northwest. This would include Washington, Oregon, Idaho, Wyoming, and Montana. This area is already inhabited by dozens of small racist and other anti-Semitic groups (Zeskind, 1987b; CDR, 1988).

WHITE AMERICAN BASTION

Robert Mathews of the Order proposed a "White American Bastion" whereby whites would migrate to the Pacific northwest. He continued this desire throughout the life of the Order and used mail order advertisements to bring in supporters (Flynn and Gerhardt, 1989). The robberies and plunder were to raise funds for his revolutionary establishment in the northwest (Ridgeway, 1990).

While this strategy for settling members from other regions is not likely to quickly establish a separate republic, it is likely to increase the potential level of violence for that region (CDR, 1988). Idaho lawmakers tried to address this problem, taking aim at white supremacist groups, introducing legislation that would prohibit terrorist acts. Richard Butler called their plan a violation of the constitutional right to bear arms (*Washington Post*, 1987). This plan also included deeding the rest of the United States to blacks and the Zionist Occupation Government (ZOG). New Mecca, formerly Chicago, would be the black capital, and ZOG's capital would be Hymietown, formerly New York City (Jordan, 1986).

The Nationalist Socialist Vanguard, formerly of Salinas, CA, has moved to the Dalles, Oregon, and Goldendale, Washington, areas and seeks to build a neo-Nazi community called Wolf Stadt (ADL, 1988a).

Kim Badynski, who previously led one of the few major Klan factions outside the south, which was in Chicago, has left that area to move to Washington state with the Northwest Knights of the KKK. He is only one of the right wing leaders who have migrated there (ADL, 1988a; Suall and Lowe, 1987).

CHAPTER XIV

Theological Basis for Racist Beliefs: Christian Identity

T he Christian Identity movement puts forth the theological basis for racism, as well as being a great unifying influence on the extreme branch of the right wing. Much of their theological beliefs have already been discussed in Chapter IX. Christian Identity was founded in the late 18th Century by an unbalanced man called Richard Brothers, who could have paralleled the "unbalanced personality" of the typology. He prophesied that on a certain date in 1795, God would come down from Heaven and proclaim Brothers to be "prince of the Hebrews."

This did not happen, but Brothers and his followers decided that Jews could not be the remnants of the Biblical nation of Israel. They decided that actually they were the true lost tribe, and Brother's teaching invested Aryans with a Biblical mantle of righteousness that the Jews were usurping their heritage with their claim of being the Chosen people. Edward Hine formalized this theory in 1871.

Christian Identity teaching was largely forgotten for a century until it was renewed in the days of the civil rights movement by a volatile Methodist minister named Wesley Swift. He added his own tenets to the Christian Identity doctrine (Martinez and Guinther, 1988).

Identity theory teaches that the United States, not Israel, is God's promised land, and that non-white races are pre-Adamic, part of the Creation that God finished before he created Adam, and these subhuman non-whites were sent outside Eden before the creation of Adam and Eve. When Eve disobeyed God, she was implanted with both Adam's seed and that of the serpent Satan. All were then cast out of Eden, and eternal racist conflict was decreed (Ridgeway, 1990).

Identity believers are given a religious basis for racism and an ideological basis for violence against minorities. This religious and theological basis provides the backbone for much of the motivation of the individuals identified in the typology. They believe that at the coming of the apocalypse, the earth will be rid of the "mud people" and reserved for the true Israelite people, the white Aryans whose sign of racial purity is the ability to blush (Ridgeway, 1990).

Identity advocates despise the federal government, calling it the Zionist Occupational Government, or ZOG (Ostfing, 1986). Some Identity beliefs do not appear to originate with the Lost Tribes conflict. Robert Miles stated that his "Dualism" doctrine believes in multiple partner marriages. The Order did also, with Robert Mathews having families in both Washington and Wyoming (Scigliano, 1986). Richard Butler promised that when David Lane was released from prison, many wives would be awaiting him (Coates, 1987).

While making more a political than theological statement, the so-called patriot organizations are a semi-anarchic collection of groups devoted to a particular interpretation of the Constitution. They believe in a Christian Republic, that there is an international Jewish conspiracy, but they do not call for the extermination of those of color, but want to return to the time of Jim Crow laws (Zeskind, 1987b).

NEO-NAZI BELIEFS

Neo-Nazi theology conflicts with the ideology of Christian Identity groups in that they declare that Israelites are ancestors of the Jews and the source of all evil. This conflict, however, has not appeared to hinder cooperation between the two groups (Scigliano, 1986). Some neo-Nazi groups worship Norse gods, as discussed earlier.

POSSE COMITATUS

Posse doctrine differs from Identity theology in one key way, although the Posse is actually a part of the greater Christian Identity movement. Identity zealots derive their theology from religion, and urge members to prepare for the impending apocalypse, while the Posse often focuses on legal technicalities while warning of imminent collapse from either nuclear attack or economic disaster (Coates, 1987).

Leonard Zeskind of the Center for Democratic Renewal probably put it best when he says that Christian Identity "provides religious unity for differing racist political groups and brings religious people into contact with the racist movement" (Ostfing, 1986, p. 74).

The "Christian Posse" as Posse Comitatus adherents call themselves, combines the racist religious beliefs of Christian Identity with arcane notions of the Constitution. The Posse sees the U. S. as a Christian Republic, not a democracy (Smith, 1987).

CITIZEN MILITIAS

The newest type of group seen on the right wing horizon, consists of a series of citizen militias, organized in perhaps a majority of the states of the Union, and with perhaps a loose national affiliation. They have not stated definite religious affiliations, other than Christian notions. They have many of the same political ideas as the Posse Comitatus and other "patriot" groups with many of them believing that no law enforcement official higher than the county sheriff has the authority to exercise control over them.

Individuals who have connections to these militias have been involved in various acts of violence and these militias hold rallies and state their willingness to take armed action if they believe their constitutional rights are violated. The gun control lobby of the early 1990's was like throwing kerosene on this movement and helped it gain support and members from people who might have been unlikely candidates for such organizations otherwise.

CHAPTER XV

Sophisticated Communications and Technology

Right wing groups have grown to include many former military personnel and often law enforcement people. These groups are not a poorly educated group of hicks, as many previously thought of the "weekend warrior" concept of them running around their own land in camos on the weekends with their cohorts. The right wing movement is well armed and has very sophisticated communications equipment, the best that money can buy or perhaps that can be borrowed from military storehouses.

COMPUTER WARFARE

During the 1983 planning meeting at the Aryan Nations Congress, part of the planning revolved around a secure nation-wide computer system to allow the extremists to communicate among various groups. The leaders made plans for high tech warfare (*Time*, 1987a). Right wing extremist groups have made extensive use of computer bulletin boards to further their goals. They have also used other electronic media, including public access cable television, video and audio cassettes, and telephone hotlines.

An Internal Revenue Service intelligence report details a computer network run out of the West Virginia home of a Louis Beam relative, available to anyone with a home computer and telephone hook-ups. The IRS report described Louis Beam, Jr.,as a "violent, anti-Semitic ambassador-at-large" for the Aryan Nations "a church-based white supremacist movement."

The IRS is concerned about the threat posed to its employees. The report states that the danger posed by the Identity movement lies not in the size of its membership but in its use of religious themes to advocate bigotry and promote violence. The report linked the Identity movement to the KKK, Aryan Nations, Posse Comitatus and Christian Defense League (Anderson and Spears, 1986). Louis Beam is formerly of the United Klans of America, the Texas KKK, and went on to become Ambassador-at-Large to the Aryan Nations (Martinez and Guinther, 1988).

COMPUTER BULLETIN BOARDS

By 1987, Beam had created at least a dozen racist computerized bulletin boards, some ultrasecret and others relatively public, which right wing groups could use to communicate over telephone and modem through software supplied by Beam (Coates, 1987).

The newest form of mass communication is these electronic "bulletin boards." They are cheaper, more accessible, and have less regulation than nearly any other national medium. Several million Americans can hook up to bulletin boards from their homes, in addition to those who have access to a computer system at work. The right wing extremists use the Aryan Nations Liberty Net, and other such networks, their own computer bulletin boards, to put out hate messages (Reid, 1985).

WHO POLICES CYBERSPACE?

The lack of controls or even knowledge on how to control computer bulletin boards has been seen recently in the sophisticated use of the same for child pornography purposes. Those using computer systems are often better schooled than the law enforcement people chasing them and in some instances, law enforcement people have faced sanctions for invading their privacy and their rights. This has occurred when law enforcement officials have tried to track child pornographers in cyberspace and ended up crashing because they invaded computer space that also occupied confidential business records and other things not having to do with illegal activities. It is such a new area that computer experts for the right wing or others can mostly write their own ticket and it is only now that law enforcement is looking for a legal and sensible way to monitor them.

After the Oklahoma bombing, even the most outspoken advocates of free speech seemed determined to censor those who misuse computer "space," by disseminating bomb making manuals and other mass destruction information. Senate hearings in May 1995 noted that hate groups and paramilitary organizations have been using computers for years to communicate with each other. Information available online includes information on how to make a better bomb than the Oklahoma City bomb, books on bomb making, and instructions on where to buy ammonium nitrate to make bombs (Hall, 1995).

GETTING OUT THE MESSAGE

In the aftermath of the Oklahoma City bombing, right wing computer bulletin boards were buzzing with theories that the U. S. government had caused the disaster to throw suspicion on right wing groups. It would give them more freedom in investigating the groups and more ease in passing gun control laws.

The Aryan Nations Liberty Net is available for a $5 subscription fee and lists ZOG (Zionist Occupation Government) informers and offers editiorials. Glenn Miller stated, "It's a tremendous tool in the awakenings of the white Christian people to the Jewish plot to destroy the white race and Christianity." He went on to say that because of the "Jewish controlled mass media, we have to take our messages directly to the people" (*Newsweek*, 1984, p. 20). These messages to the people have occasionally included death sentences to such ZOG figures as Morris Dees, head of the Southern Poverty Law Center, always a thorn in the side of white extremist groups (Martinez and Guinther, 1988). This death sentence for Dees is called up under the heading, "Morris Dees Queer" (Coates, 1987, p. 65). "Know Your Enemies" provides lists of ZOG informants and Communists (*Newsweek*, 1984).

There are various computerized networks available to like-minded white activists from all over the country. The first has already been mentioned, the Aryan Nations Liberty Net, set up by Louis Beam. Another major network is operated by George

Dietz of West Virginia, a farm broker and publisher of white supremacist materials. His bulletin board is called Info International (ADL, 1985a).

A USEFUL TOOL

According to the Anti-Defamation League of B'nai B'rith (ADL, 1985a), enemy lists on this system can only be accessed with what is called "level seven" clearance. These bulletin boards serve the hate movement in several ways. First, they are able to spread the hate propaganda among young people since many computer "hackers" are the young. Secondly, they are able to bypass a closely enforced embargo on the importation of hate literature into Canada (ADL, 1985a). This bypass of official scrutiny and law enforcement may be likened to the messages that child pornographers put on the"entry" to their computer programs, telling the caller if they are police, feds, or the like that there are materials contained therein which constitute legal business. It is an area in which courts and legislation have not outlined what is constitutionally acceptable and what is not.

Third, the groups are able to stir up hatred against those whom the groups consider their enemies. Lastly, this medium offers a potential for circulating coded messages among like minded right wing activitists (ADL, 1985a), using security clearances and code words to keep out those who should not have access. This potential for providing instantaneous communications to coordinate terrorist actions was not available to Bob Mathews and the Order but is available now (Martinez and Guinther, 1988) and is being widely used.

Tom Metzger, another white supremacist pioneer in computer and video technology, used his group, the White Aryan Resistance (WAR) to set up another computer bulletin board accessible to the general public. Within the bulletin board was a semi-secret section for private correspondence between a smaller group of users (Zeskind, 1987b).

CABLE TELEVISION

In addition to bulletin boards, right wing extremist groups have also taken to the air in the form of cable television programs.

Dwight McCarthy, white supremacist, hosted the "Aryan Nations Hour" on KZZI television near Salt Lake City, Utah. There was great outrage in the community about how the freedom of speech right was being used (*Time*, 1987b).

Tom Metzger is the guru of television personalities among those more accustomed to wearing hoods. His cable television program, "Race and Reason" draws a white supremacist audience, and he has also appeared on nationally syndicated programs (ADL, 1987a). Tom Metzger has also announced his support for black activist Louis Farrakhan who also used public access television to stir up hatred against Jews.

In 1991, there were as many as fifty-seven "hate shows" across the country. In addition to "Race and Reason," there was "Airlink" which comes from Mississippi and presents a more sedate viewpoint. Richard Barrett, a New York-born attorney, runs the program and is the head of the right wing "Nationalist Movement." He has filed many lawsuits over roadblocks put in the way of his cable television path. Hate shows have First Amendment protection and the 1987 Cable Communications Policy Act requires public access channels be uncensored except for obscenity (Zoglin, 1993).

William Pierce, although in an isolated and fairly unsophisticated part of the country, operates a regularly heard radio program heard on AM and shortwave stations all over the country. He is technologicaly sophiscated and since power outages are not uncommon in the West Virginia mountains, he probably has generators and methods to supply his own electricity when needed.

AUDIO AND VIDEO CASSETTES

Home video cassettes are used to allow the faithful and potential converts to watch programs on their home televisions starring leaders such as the Posse's Jim Wickstrom or Louis Beam. Audio cassettes of Identity sermons are available by Gale, Butler, Thom Robb, and others who spread the message. Telephone "hot lines" also allow interested parties to call and hear the latest conspiracy theories (Coates, 1987).

This widespread use of video cassettes has been seen with the recent surge of videos distributed by the state militias to spread their message. One video, in particular, called "America in Peril" details what militia members believe is the actions of the federal government in setting up the "New World Order" and allowing the United Nations to take over the rule of the United States. The tape shows the location where the militia believes there will be concentration camps set up in the United States with U. N. troops and former street gangs trained as soldiers to keep the peace.

Other sections of the video detail how the federal government launched offensive action on a group of law abiding, gun toting Christians at Waco, Texas, and murdered them. Another section shows a speaker who accuses Janet Reno of being lesbian, of being stopped for drunken driving, and other transgressions. Much of the material does not support the conspiracy theory being put forth. This is the type of material given out, however. This particular video was distributed in southern Illinois in 1994.

What is very interesting about this video, however, is the fact that the speaker for the first two parts of the tape is "Mark from Michigan," identified by national news as Mark Koernke, from the Michigan Militia. The Michigan Militia disclaimed any knowledge of the bombing in Oklahoma City or any connection with Timothy McVeigh, but he appeared to have at least attended Militia meetings.

RADIO TALK SHOWS

Radio talk shows have also become a outlet for right wing rhetoric. President Clinton recently attacked conservative talk show hosts for their inflammatory rhetoric of hate, calling them "purveyors of hate" on the "airwaves" (*Time*, 1995, p. 35) in the wake of the Oklahoma City bombings. Clinton said, "They spread hate. They leave the impression, that by their very words, violence is acceptable (*Post Dispatch*, April 25, 1995).

President Clinton stated, "We hear so many loud and angry voices in America today whose sole goal seems to be to try to keep some people as paranoid as possible and the rest of us all torn up and upset with each other" in a speech in Minneapolis in

April 1995. He said that the hate messages over radio, TV, and computers may have helped push "fragile" people who may have extreme views over the edge.

It is not even the more violent and marginal agents such as Mark Koernke, and others who are seen as a bit offbeat, however, with the antigovernment message. G. Gordon Liddy, well known for Watergate and host of the nation's second most widely heard talk show, allegedly told his listeners about shooting for the heads of federal agents who invade their homes because of their bullet-proof vests. He then reconsidered the next day because the head is harder to hit and told them to shoot twice to the body or for the groin (Lacayo, 1995).

Gordon Liddy gave his own version of what he had said to *Soldier of Fortune* magazine in July 1995 and it is reported in the October 1995 issue. He claims that what he said was taken out of context and he was used as a scapegoat by President Clinton for media attention. Liddy states that his radio statements were subsequent to an editiorial in *Modern Gun* by Jim Shults in which Mr. Shults was alleging that some people were so incensed at BATF for their abuses that they were advocating hunting them down and killing them as if they were Viet Cong. Liddy states he was concerned about this backlash and stated on the air, over two hundred and sixty or so radio stations, that it is not warranted to go out and actively hunt people down to kill them.

Liddy alleges that what he said about shooting them was, "I can forsee circumstances when these totally out-of-control BATF people come in the middle of the night, smash your door down without any notice whatsoever and come in shooting. Then, you have a choice. You can either let yourself get killed or you can defend yourself and shoot back. I said, of course if you're going to shoot back and whack these sons of bitches, remember that they're wearing flak jackets, head shots, etc" (Brown, 1995, 73). Liddy said that there had been no criticism of him when he made the statements in August 1994, but because the White House wanted to imply an association the like of those who did the bombing in Oklahoma City, they dusted off his comments to bring out recently.

There is no easy answer as to who is right and who is wrong and what should be said and what should not be said. Probably the best answer is honesty and using the statements in the spirit and context in which they are made. Freedom of speech is one of our most important freedoms and infringements should not be made on freedom of speech unless statements are such that they cause imminent threats to the life and liberty of others.

On the other hand, when anti-government sentiment goes so far as to encourage violence against law enforcement officials and public figures, and is applauded by talk show hosts and other national speakers and politicians, it gives extremists permission to conclude that terrorism is just one more form of noble resistance to tyranny (Lacayo, 1995). They can see their actions, even killing young children in Oklahoma City, as patriotic and just.

This takes a page out of Andrew Macdonald AKA William Pierce's *The Turner Diaries* in which violent and inhuman actions are seen as just and reasonable to restore the country to its white beginnings. Any one with sentiments favoring association with blacks, anyone who had supported blacks in public housing or any civil rights manuvers, and anyone with similar associations with Jews, was killed in as public a manner as possible, to get the point across (Macdonald, 1980).

CHAPTER XVI

Paramilitary and Survivalist Training

P aramilitary training has become a standard of right wing extremist groups, with some of them doing standard military drills and the more covert groups being involved with automatic weapons and high explosives. This training includes not only this more obvious aspect, but also the gathering of information about enemies of the "cause." This began with the Minutemen and continues with the groups today. The Order had a hit list of government officials and prominent Jews, including Alan Berg, who was gunned down for his talk show rhetoric against right wingers.

This paramilitary and survivalist training has become more standard with the advent of unorganized citizen militias in the mid-1990's. Legislation was passed in the 1980's banning paramilitary training and automatic weapons training in several states. This has not prevented some of the more militant groups from finding locations where such training can be done and doing it secretly.

THE MINUTEMEN

The idea of defending their beliefs in an organized military manner began with the Minutemen, which operated in a fashion which any military organization might appreciate. Their intelligence system, paramilitary field training, security system, and stockpiling of food and other necessities may have helped set the pattern for today's violent right wing extremist groups.

The Minutemen operated using many strategies normally associated with military planning. The members were basically trained as soldiers, but part-time soldiers, who would activate when needed to serve and protect their country. The Minutemen used intelligence gathering to target their enemies and other secuirty measures in an effort to safeguard their security. Despite their efforts, their security was often breached and the group was thorougly infiltrated.

CITIZEN MILITIAS

Today's groups have many prior and even current military people involved. These people with prior military training and experience have access to the most up to date and sophisticated gadgetry, weapons, and communications. They have the training needed to use these items and are already accustomed to military discipline and organization.

More recently, citizen militias have begun with members mostly white males who do weekend drills, dressed in camoflage with various weaponry, practicing survival skills. The militias have attracted many members with prior military experience and those with previous associations with various right wing groups.

Many militia members are simply loyal Americans upset with the direction they see their country headed. Problems arise when they are led into illegal acts by those with more extreme views or when someone who joins the group already has psychotic tendencies and takes the ideas and runs with them in a direction that leads to disaster.

These citizen militias practice military drills and military discipline at the time they are participating in the group. The militias, rather than defending our country from an outside enemy, are generally more geared to fighting the enemy within our borders. The militias are planning and training for long term **civil** disorder within the boundaries of this nation and many of them see the present government as the enemy of the people.

A COMMON DENOMINATOR

This paramilitary and survivalist training appears to be a common denominator to the different types of groups examined, whether KKK, neo-Nazi, Christian Identity, or the new militias. Members of various factions of the Ku Klux Klans have been charged with illegal training under paramilitary statutes. Members of the UKA were prosecuted for illegal paramilitary training as was Glenn Miller of the White Patriot Party.

Christian Identity groups which include the Order, CSA, Aryan Nations, Posse, and other Christian Patriot groups are rooted in the belief that they must prepare for the battle of Armageddon. These groups often have specialists in various aspects of military training, such as Randall Rader and Richard Scutari of the CSA, who were, respectively, experts in paramilitary training and martial arts. It is because of this belief in the impending apocalypse or Armageddon that they believe will occur in this country before the end of this century that the groups can justify arming themselves, stockpiling weapons and learning survivalism.

ROOTS OF CONSPIRACY

During the 1983 Aryan Nations World Congress, CSA leaders Jim Ellison and Kerry Noble agreed that their compound would be used for guerilla warfare training. The CSA role would be to supervise paramilitary training to carry out strikes against Jewish businesses and assassinate federal officials (Bishop, 1988). As has already been stated, the CSA was well prepared to coordinate such training.

Randall Rader was the dean of paramilitary training instructors, and after he joined the Order, he trained the members like some sort of Olympic coach, training them in marksmanship and commando tactics. As a moneymaker for the CSA, he had previously taught courses throughout the Midwest and South where he demonstrated weapons use and advertised guns made at the CSA compound. Rader also helped conduct a military boot-style camp at the CSA compound, called the "End Time Overcomer Survival Training School" for which outsiders paid $500 for the privilege of attending. Interestingly, the "End Times" comes from a discussion in Christian fundamentalist literature which calls "end times" the time just before or during the Second Coming of Christ. This period is generally associated with social upheaval, natural disaster, pandemics, famine, and war (Zeskind,

1987a). The CSA operated a training compound called Silhouette City, where neo-Nazis commandos worked on urban battle techniques. This was set up to resemble the FBI course at Quantico, Virginia (Coates, 1987).

The CSA was not only involved in survivalist training, but had their own armory to manufacture automatic weapons. Besides the classes they held for right wing extremists, and even outside survivalists, they attended gun shows and sold weapons. They also had possession of poisonous cyanide and explosives for terrorist actions (Bishop, 1988).

FREEDOM FESTIVALS

Christian Patriots Defense League, formerly of Flora, Illinois, sponsored the "Freedom Festival" for several years. It included training events for paramilitary and survivalist training. Various other Christian Identity groups have armed followers and restrict access to the compounds where they reside. The Christian Patriots Defense League, in addition to the Illinois site, had a compound across the Arkansas border in Missouri, and a training facility in West Virginia (Coates, 1987). Johnny Bob Harrell is now elderly and has abandoned the Flora, Illinois, site to move to Missouri. Details of his current situation are not known.

ARYAN NATIONS

The Aryan Nations always have a "security chief" who is responsible for training (Martinez and Guinther, 1988) and security at the Aryan Nations compound. Neo-Nazi groups perform activities with a military air and wear uniforms and insignia reminiscent of Adolf Hitler (Coplon, 1988). These groups often participate in Christian Identity gatherings and training (ADL, 1988a).

The Aryan Nations compound is in an isolated area of Idaho. It is fenced and patrolled by armed guards. Entry is through a gate manned by an "officer" in a stormtrooper uniform.

Aryan Nations "security chiefs" have been involved in several documented arrests and criminal acts. These include Gary Yarbrough of the Order and then Elden "Bud" Cutler.

POSSE COMITATUS

The Posse Comitatus has also been very active in paramilitary training and survivalism. However, they are an ultrasecret movement, other than in a few incidents where their activities became public knowledge with Gordon Kahl and others, and their doctrine requires that Posse warriors keep their affiliations secret. That makes them the least documented of the far right. Their doctrine requires them to hoard large amounts of firearms and food to prepare for Armageddon. Available information points to the likelihood of them training in secret.

BRANCH DAVIDIANS

David Koresh had been accumulating large amounts of weaponry and food stocks, enough arms to arm the entire population of the Branch Davidian compound in Waco, Texas. He was able to purchase legal devices, such as inert hand grenades and also the ingredients to arm them and make them active. Enough food was stockpiled for the compound to be self-sufficient for a long period. When they were raided by agents of the BATF, they were able to have many Branch Davidians firing at the federal agents who invaded and hold them off.

The federal agents involved did not adequately seek intelligence information and were unaware of facts that might have prevented some of the lost lives at Waco. The Branch Davidians were prepared for a long siege and group warfare. They appeared to have been waiting on the federal agents and were not taken by surprise at the beginning as the agents intended.

MAIL ORDER MAYHEM

"Burn and blow" books are popular and easily available through dozens of mail order outlets. Sometimes, the person using the supplies has already had extensive training provided by the United States government, in military service. The Oklahoma City bombing appeared to be done by someone who had some knowledge of where to place the explosives, familiarity with the amount needed to do the job, and how to cause the explosion and get away safely.

Timothy McVeigh, one of the men accused in the bombing, was arrested in a routine traffic stop. A reasonable person might have questions about why he was arrested so easily and did not make better plans to avoid police attention, and if he might have placed himself in a position to be arrested to further the cause by stating his case in court when the matter goes to trial.

Timothy McVeigh had received extensive military training in the U. S. Army. He had even tried to get into Special Forces training and seemed to have more training and expertise than most ordinary soldiers.

CHAPTER XVII

Summary and Conclusions

Definite patterns of changes have been documented in the types of armed violence toward the U. S. government and selected minorities in the past quarter of a century and this level of violence has escalated. Right wing groups with historically different roots but similar goals have begun to work together and even consolidate to further their goals and interests. Identifying characteristics of the various types of individuals within these groups is useful in understanding their motivaitons and the roles they play within the organization. That is why the typology was developed and used.

Examing the several factors that make these groups unique provides another type of framework for understanding them. Several factors, including the historical background, have been examined.

WHERE DID THEY COME FROM?
JOHN BIRCH SOCIETY

Many right wing extremists had their beginnings with the more benign John Birch Society (see Appendix A). Some of these members moved on to the more militant Minutemen and the Minutemen may have served as a pattern and inspiration for the groups that followed. Robert B. DePugh of the Minutemen, and Bob Mathews and Richard Scutari of the Order are only a few of those who began with the John Birch Society.

The John Birch Society started out with intentions of being a patriotic American organization to fight communism. They do not make public statements about anti-Semitism. At times, they have been abandoned by more extreme right wing militants for their more moderate stance.

KU KLUX KLANS

The Ku Klux Klan began initially because of southern dissatisfaction at the hands of northern politicians in the wake of the Civil War. The land had been raped and pillaged by "carpetbaggers" from the north and thieving southerners called "scalawags." Six young Confederate soldiers found their own way of diversion and a way to fight back. This became the roots of the Klans of today.

Historically, the Ku Klux Klan promoted violence against blacks, and then immigrants. During various times in history, the Klans have been very influential in state and even national politics. They have held political and law enforcement offices in various southern states and prevented the prosecution of southerners for offenses against blacks.

They went on to expand their activities to pursue activities against various minorities, particularly Jews. As the Klans began to get hit in the purse with civil suits over members they had coached and who committed crimes, they began a campaign of salesmanship and talked about their changed image. This image, however, was for appearances only as they climbed into bed with the Aryan Nations and other Christian Identity groups.

The Ku Klux Klan is not one group as the public generally thinks of "the Klan," but rather is three national organizations and a multitude of smaller, sometimes unaffiliated branches. The three national organizations are the United Klans of America, the Invisible Empire, Knights of the Ku Klux Klan, and the Knights of the Ku Klux Klan. The various Klan factions have different priorities and activities, and generally do not cooperate with each other. The Klans continue to recruit, particularly the Knights of the Ku Klux Klan, who hold recruitment rallies in various states.

NEO-NAZIS

Groups emulating Hitler existed long before the neo-Nazi groups of today. The Silver Shirts began here in the 1930's and some of the later neo-Nazis were involved with the Silver Shirts, including Gerald L. K. Smith of the Christian Nationalist Church and Henry Beach of the Posse Comitatus. Wesley Swift was Gerald L. K. Smith's right hand man and Swift became acquainted with Richard Butler. It was Swift and Butler who organized the Christian Defense League in the 1970's, which may help explain why the Aryan Nations is more of a hybrid organization. One only needs to look at Richard Butler's beginnings.

The American Nazi Party was the first group to gain nationwide attention and membership. George Lincoln Rockwell is still a familiar name to many. Neo-Nazi groups have fallen on hard times and their numbers have decreased. However, their activities have also changed. They have begun coordinating their efforts with Christian Identity and Aryan Nations groups, despite their differing theologies or lack of the same. The Aryan Nations is really a hybrid organization consisting of components of neo-Nazi ideas and Christian Identity.

Some groups associated with neo-Nazi beliefs have had more success. William Pierce is a leader of the right wing extremist movement and with an alleged transfer of funds from the Order, he established a new compound for his followers in West Virginia.

William Pierce operates from an isolated base in the West Virginia mountains, having relocated there from Washington, D. C. Pierce was formerly involved with the National Youth Alliance and Willis Carto.

Pierce's influence is nationwide via short wave and AM radio broadcasts, as well as a wealth of published material, and computer networking. One of his publications, *The Turner Diaries,* has been attributed to be the inspiration for two major events involving many victims. The first was the Order whose crime spree ranged from murders to counterfeiting to robbery of an armored vehicle. The second was the largest mass murder in United States history, the bombing of the federal building in Oklahoma City.

Pierce discounts the idea that his book is the inspiration for the bombing and says that he has no control over who reads his book. He does indicate that he believes this is only a harbinger of things to come as people are dissatisfied with the government and the government takes illegal actions against its citizens.

William Pierce is an influential figure nationwide and there are indications that he may be planning a more central role in theright wing movement. There has never been one central national organization and leadership with the various right wing extremist groups. With so many different groups, different ideas, and different agendas, it is unlikely that they can all come to agree on anything but even with partial organization, they could become a dangerous threat if their past activities continue and they develop a central planning organization.

Tom Metzger and the White Aryan Resistance, while they have had their ups and downs, are still a viable group. Tom Metzger pioneered cable television as a way to get out his message. He has also been influential in organizing skinhead groups and others, particularly youth groups with a white supremacy message.

Other neo-Nazi groups have not had this success. There are also those who are involved with these groups but stay at the legal fringes, such people as Willis Carto and his Liberty Lobby, a powerful political force in Washington.

SKINHEADS

Skinhead groups began in the mid-1980's in this country. They are best known for their violent activities against whoever they decide is "the enemy." The standard for such groups is the maximum amount of violence and intimidation they can inflict.

Skinhead groups have become involved with other right wing groups and have been the"muscle" insome instances. They have committed crimes for which other right wing groups have been sued civilly because of the influence they exerted over the skinhead groups.

CHRISTIAN IDENTITY

The Identity movement consists of loose bands of Christian Patriots who have their roots in Anglo-Israelism, which identified Anglo-Saxons as the Ten Lost Tribes of Israel. Christian Identity groups have continued the evolution of this theological message and further refined it, pointing to white Anglo-Saxon Americans as the true "chosen people," not the Jews. Christian Identity groups have been told to prepare for the coming of Armageddon and this is a central tenet of their doctrine. They have become involved in paramilitary training, survivalism, and various forms of civil disobedience. They have begun to switch to propaganda and political action, a perfect setting for the Christian Identity movement.

Christian Identity adherents have made use of the mass media to distribute their message via television and audio cassettes. This use of mass media is not limited merely to the major groups. Smaller groups have also used video and audio cassettes. A small group in southern Illinois called "Heirs of theBlessing" have distributed what a local pastor calls "God squad" messages via audio cassettes. The Michigan militia and other militias have distributed audio and video cassettes advocating armed action against the government if the government takes certain actions. They have also made widespread use of computer bulletin boards.

"MINUTEMEN" AND MILITIAS

Right wing extremists are best described as "minutemen" who are ready to fight at a moment's notice. This "minuteman" concept has been very important to the right wing movement historically and is very important to it today. The "Minutemen" were the forefather of many of these modern groups and the more organized and effective of the modern groups have taken note of the Minutemen strategies. Similar to the organization of the Minutemen, the Order used a secret cell structure, paramilitary training, and code names.

The various militias who are operating partially covertly have apparently adapted the Minutemen's secret "cell" structure, military techniques in weaponry, survivalist training, and intelligence gathering, and are able to conduct their activities while avoiding government scrutiny in many cases. This "secret cell" theory was further refined by Robert Miles in 1987 who compared the concept to a spider web which, when invaded, is still there when the threat is withdrawn.

Citizen militias are operating in the majority of the states of the United States, often with several branches in various parts of the state. Some of them are active in more than one state and have made efforts at national organization. The militias do not have one common platform or "constitution." Some of them use the "Articles of Confederation" as their constitution, predating the federal constitution and wanting to replace it with the previous document. Some of them rely on language designating "unorganized militias" in every state to defend the nation.

While there is no one common theme, there are several themes that have common threads in the rhetoric. Conspiracy themes abound, dealing with "one world government" and a conspiracy by the United Nations to take over this country. This will be done by Russian troops on American soil, Chinese street gangs coming here to disarm the American public, secret "black" helicopters spying on right wing groups, and several other widely distributed conspiracy theories.

While in some instances, parts of these ideas are true, no one has come forth with proof of the conspiracies. There are black helicopters and there have been Russian tanks that the military says were used to train **our** troops to defend against them. However, how all of this fits together into the well organized conspiracy theory that will allow for a "one world government" by the year 2000 is a bit more shaky.

The militia movement has created an enigma for federal law enforcement. Because of the several recent disasters involving government agents and right wing groups, some militia members have set the stage for new confrontations by refusing to allow warrants to be served on them. There are several standoffs at present where law enforcement officials will not take action for fear of another violent confrontation, lost lives, and the public scrutiny that would be caused.

April 19 has become the Ides of March to the right wing extremist movement. That date is significant due to the Waco incident and now, the Oklahoma City bombing, as well as other actions that have occurred on that date.

The militia movement has spawned its own cottage industry. That is one of distributing video and audio cassettes with messages about the "Waco conspiracy," Janet Reno, and general dissatisifaction with the U. S. government. Mark Koernke, the now famous "Mark from Michigan" on the tapes came from the Michigan Militia to spread his message of dire threats of destruction and conspiracy.

PRINCIPALS OF THE "MOVEMENT"

Richard Butler of the Aryan Nations is one of the best known Identity leaders, although his group is more of a hybrid and encompasses elements of neo-Nazi doctrine and insignia, as well as Christian Identity. He established the Church of Jesus Christ-Christian and the Aryan Nations at Hayden Lake, Idaho, in the 1970's. He hosts Congresses that allow right wing extremists from all over the country and even from other countries, and from a variety of persuasions to get together. He is closely allied with Louis Beam, who has ties to the Texas KKK. Butler promotes ties between his group, Klan factions, Christian Identity groups, skinheads, and any other white supremacy groups who care to align. He is also active in prison ministries, recruiting "Aryan warriors" within the prison walls, to join the group upon their release from prison.

Robert Miles operated the Mountain Church in Cohoctaw, Michigan, until his death and was a principal of the Identity movement. He was known as a "thinker" of the movement and advocated that the five states of the Pacific northwest be set aside for a white American homeland.

Miles was also involved in prison ministries. He actively recruited other right wing groups and believed in a return to secrecy involving activities of the groups. He developed a "secret cell" idea by which the contamination or termination of one group would allow the others to continue their activities without security being breached.

Robert Jay Mathews made history after he left the National Alliance and associated with Aryan Nations and KKK adherents to begin a group called the Order or Silent Brotherhood. It was the first time in this century that a right wing group took direct action to overturn the U. S. government. The group attempted to bankroll a white American homeland, similar to that envisioned by other right wing leaders.

Robert Mathews recruited members with various military specialties, much as is done with elite military forces. He recruited those with weaponry expertise, personal defense tactics, intelligence gathering, financing (and counterfeiting), and other specialties. The Order ran a major counterfeiting ring, robbed a Brinks car for $3.6 million dollars, committed at least three murders, and has the distinction of taking in the largest haul in history. Robert Mathews' acts are still unparalleled in organizing a secret paramilitary force and taking action against the United States government. How he was able to launch such a massive conspiracy and carry out many of the actions shows the organization and level of activities among the groups. This was **before** most of the extensive efforts made by Aryan Nations and others to establish nationwide secure computer bulletin boards.

The Posse Comitatus began in 1969 as a loose band of vigilantes and survivalists that believed that any law enforcement and government agency above the county level operates illegally. They do not believe that federal taxation is legal and many refuse to pay taxes.

Posse members, such as Gordon Kahl, have had shootouts with federal agents and other law enforcement officers assisting them, who have tried to enforce federal laws and tax collection. Posse members keep their membership secret and stockpile weapons, also emulating the Minutemen. The Posse also took a page out of the Minutemen training book and rigged their computer information to self destruct to avoid it falling into enemy hands when the National Commodities and Barter Exchange was raided. More recently, Posse groups have encouraged members to use alternative currencies to pay off debts.

Other Christian Identity groups such as the Covenant, the Sword, and the Arm of the Lord (CSA) have had a major impact on the right wing extremist movement. CSA members were very active in training and then hiding members of the Order. Also closely allied is the Christian Patriots Defense League, an umbrella group for other patriot groups, which has been active in paramilitary training.

There are numerous small churches and congregations which comprise the "Christian Identity" movement. Several of the groups have been involved in violence, including the Arizona Patriots and Church of the Creator. Other groups have had supporters who became involved in violent activities.

Pete Peters' Church of Christ was in an inflammatory battle with Alan Berg before Berg's death. Zillah Craig, whose mother was involved in Berg's death, met David Lane, and through him, Robert Mathews at this church. She later had Mathews' child. The Church of Israel, led by Dan Gayman, also had members who were involved with the Order. David Tate, serving a life sentence for the murder of a Missouri state trooper during the Order's activities, was reportedly a member of this church and grand jury testimony indicated that the Church of Israel was given money from the Order's crime spree,

Even after the Order was history, the Bruder Schweigen Strike Force II, the Arizona Patriots, and the Committee of the States continued violent activities in the same manner as the Order. Members of this group were arrested and charged for their violent activities.

Various Identity churches helped split the bounty from the Order's crime spree. They continue to support the right wing extremist movement and become involved with various groups and support them in their right wing ideas.

William Pierce heads the National Alliance, now located in a remote area of West Virginia. He had much recent media attention with the Oklahoma City bombing and allegations that the event was patterned after an incident in his book, *The Turner Diaries*. He is one of the leaders in the forefront of the right wing movement and is the intellectual leader.

CONSPIRATORIAL ACTIVITIES AMONG GROUPS

The interconnections and conspiracy among the various groups have been shown extensively, with the Order being the clearest example of the extent and sophistication of the interconnections. These groups work together on an everyday basis, however, attending each other's training, assisting in providing hideouts, and in other activities. The most recent of these is political action, even running for political office with a right wing platform.

The Klans and neo-Nazis have been invited and participated in gatherings at Robert Miles' Mountain Church in Cohoctah, Michigan; Aryan Nations Congresses at Hayden Lake, Idaho; and at John Harrell's Freedom Festivals and survivalist training in Flora, Illinois, the Arkansas-Missouri border, and in an isolated area of West Virginia.

The Aryan Nations Congresses have helped spawn support for Gordon Kahl and the birth of the Order. William Pierce attended the 1995 Congress, possibly in an effort to further unite and organize the various right wing groups in this country.

The Order not only was made up of members from several groups, but their booty was distributed to several organizations of several different persuasions. The FBI was able to recover only a fraction of the money from the crime spree. Members of the Order were hidden by various groups and then secreted away to other locations when authorities got too close, speaking to a sophisticated communications and intelligence network.

Various Christian Identity groups have been involved in learning to acquire tax exempt status by operating under the mantle of a church. More recently was the concept of "fractional reserve notes," funny money used to pay off credit card and bank loans debts. The National Commodities and Barter Exchange was also a well thought out and unique way to avoid federal income taxes and other regulations, operating an entire bank still based on silver bullion.

Lands rights' groups have evolved in the western states. They have been suspected in the bombing of the office of forest rangers in Carson City, Nevada. These groups have also been attracted to the dialogue of the new citizen militias and have taken up some of their conspiracy-style ideas.

EPISODES OF VIOLENCE

While the Klan's history of murdering blacks spanned more than a century, their level of violence fell sharply during the-1960's, and the episodes of violence were more sporadic and generally smaller scale. Some of the violent incidents helped cause the downfall of particular Klans to near obscurity, such as the United Klans incident where members hanged a black teenager. This caused a civil lawsuit and led the way for groups that monitor and battle extreme right wing groups to develop another weapon against them - civil lawsuits.

Neo-Nazi groups were small and largely quiet during the same period. The early 1970's saw left wing violence escalate more than any right wing group could muster. That changed, however, and neo-Nazi right wing involvement became greater and often changed to a more hybrid involvement with groups such as the Aryan Nations. More "pure" neo-Nazi groups also associated with other types of groups in their violence.

Several new right wing extremist groups began in the 1970's and started growing in size and strength, changing the direction of extremist violence. KKK violence surged upward again and the targets become more varied. Skinheads came to America in the 1980's. Skinheads have become involved with several other groups in violent episodes. They have been involved with the White Aryan Resistance and perpetrated a homicide that caused another large civil lawsuit. More recently, skinhead groups have become involved in anti-abortion protests. This seem likely to be connected to some of their prior contacts with Christian Identity and other extremist right wing elements.

Christian Identity emerged from the shadows to cover the Midwest landscape with newspapers detailing the martyrdom of Gordon Kahl and details of the Christian Identity and Posse Comitatus movement.

The shootout with Gordon Kahl, his flight from federal officers, and his eventual fiery death became a rallying point for right wing extremists. This was the first of the well publicized cases where federal agents were criticized for not using available intelligence information that told them that their plan of action with the man they were trying to arrest would not work. The agents were warned that he would resist arrest and would do so violently. This showdown has been the subject of movies and police training subsequent to the event.

The Order was created and began a reign of violence that included the largest Brinks robbery in history, several deaths, and plans to shut down a major city through terrorism. The Order accomplished more violence and mayhem than any group since the Minutemen. Their prospective hit list would have grayed the hair of many prominent politicians on the list and city planners for cities where they planned massive destruction. Even after the Order's demise, other members of the original groups tried to revive the Order as the Bruder Schweigen Strike Force II, which was short lived but very violent.

Members of Christian Identity groups and the Posse are encouraged to stockpile weapons and prepare for the final battle of Armageddon. Gordon Kahl and other tax protestors have resorted to violence against federal officers. Forestry officers in the western United States are afraid to go into the forest alone due to threats of violence and the recent bombing of a forestry office.

Other individuals have formed their own survivalist groups after becoming acquainted with the right wing extremist position. Some of the individuals were psychotic and violent and have committed unspeakable acts against their followers and the general public, in the name of their cause, whatever that might be. While the organized groups do not condone them, their inspiration and permission to use force did come from that source. They take some of the more common ideas, add their own twists, and believe they are acting as messengers of God.

David Koresh and the Branch Davidians have become a rallying point for citizen militias, the Posse, and other right wing groups. Even those who did not agree with his thoughts and believe he was actually a psychopath, defend his right to be a psychopathic religious figure and have numerous guns in his compound, pointing out that the mere possession of those guns did not give the federal government reason to go into his compound. They believe that David Koresh had a right to pursue his own religious beliefs in whatever manner he chose. Those who chose to use Koresh as a martyr tend to overlook the allegations of child abuse and manipulation of the adults on the compound. Evidence does not point to this being the primary reason for the original raid, however.

The more extreme right wing groups point to a federal conspiracy at Waco, Texas, against the Branch Davidians, and insist that the federal government went in on the first day and attacked the compound without provocation, and later destroyed the compound to destroy evidence of their mistakes. The siege at Waco and the deaths of the Branch Davidians, including several children, has become one of the major arguments against federal law enforcement abuses used by right wing extremists. Then, along came Randy Weaver.

Randy Weaver and his family were involved in a standoff with federal officials in a incident that ended with the deaths of his wife, son, and a federal marshall. Weaver was found not guilty in the marshall's death and became another rallying point for the right wing and a martyr. His situation is used to bolster the position of right wing militants in that the federal government was accused of taking action against citizens who were engaged in legal political protests and religious activities.

Randy Weaver had been accused in 1989 of selling two illegal sawed-off shotguns to a government informant. He failed to show for trial and federal marshalls staked out his home on Ruby Ridge in Idaho. Randy Weaver did sell illegal weapons, but that point is muddied because he alleges that a government informant "entrapped" him by working on him for three years to make the sale to him and when Weaver needed money for groceries, he sold the illegal weapons. Weaver alleges that federal agents set him up because they needed a "snitch" that could get into the Aryan Nations compound. When he refused to be that "snitch" they took retaliatory action, he alleges.

Randy Weaver and his children were awarded $3.1 million to settle their lawsuit involving the death of Vicki Weaver. Congressional hearings in September 1995 addressed the allegations of wrong-doing by federal agents, and allegations of a cover-up. Orders were given that armed adults "could be" or "should be" shot on sight, orders contrary to those ever previously given to federal law enforcement officers in such a situation. Hearings are dealing with the question of why Randy Weaver acquired so much law enforcement scrutiny, whether or not the shooting of Mrs. Weaver was accidental or intentional, since psychological experts had noted she could be a threat to the children if she saw no way of escape, and why the order was given to fire on people who were not an immediate threat.

Randy Weaver did wrong and was convicted on the weapons charges. However, there appears to be little doubt in this instance that federal law enforcement officials also acted wrongly and perhaps criminally. The outcome of the hearing was not available at the completion of this book.

The greatest act of mass violence ever perpetrated on American soil occurred in Oklahoma City in April 1995 with the bombing of the Alfred P. Murrah Federal Building. One hundred and sixty-nine people were killed, including more than twenty children in America's Kids Day Care, which was housed at the federal building. The cause of the bombing was tons of ammonium nitrate fertilizer parked in a Ryder truck. Although there have been arrests made and the defendants are awaiting trial, the investigation is far from done and no determination has been made whether or not it is a farther reaching conspiracy.

This bombing, following the Branch Davidian siege at Waco and the Randy Weaver siege at Ruby Ridge, Idaho, has been a great topic of discussion among right wing extremists. There have been allegations that the government itself did the bombing as an excuse to crack down and intensify spying on right wing groups. Some have applauded the bombing, although being sorrowful for the deaths of the children, saying it was an expression of protest against the tyranny of the government.

Books on bomb-making, espionage, converting weapons into automatic weapons, booby trapping, and making your own homemade high explosives have been common-place. Such information is available over the Internet and has been acquired by various right wing extremist groups and also by lone individuals who identify with the rhetoric of the right wing. The dangers involved in this are being explored by government officials and many in the right wing fear a backlash against public dissemination of materials. They fear this backlash will go much further than that and involve violations of their rights.

WHITE AMERICAN HOMELAND

The establishment of a white American homeland has long been a rallying point for some of the more active white supremacists of the right wing, whether they have their roots in the Ku

Klux Klans, neo-Nazi groups, or Christian Identity. The lastest trend in this movement is small groups of survivalists who fear the federal government and who have established their own small compounds for the safety of their group when war breaks out with the federal government. They are preparing for long term civil strife.

Various groups have intentions of establishing their own group of white extremists in one location or another, but the most favored location and one that is endorsed by major leaders of the groups is the five states of the Pacific northwest. This area would be called the "White American Bastion" (Flynn and Gerhardt, 1989), or "White Aryan Republic." The idea itself was endorsed at an Aryan Nations Congress as the "Northwest Territorial Imperative" (ADL, 1988a).

Groups such as the Order have made efforts to bankroll this new nation. They planned to deed the remainder of the United States to blacks and the Jewish, each in their own part of the country, far away from the white homeland.

While there are right wing extremist groups in various parts of the country, and some of the neo-Nazi groups, in particular, are in the more eastern parts of the country, the concentration of those who are interested in a separatist nation are in that far corner of the country in the northwest. There are several reasons for this being their choice location. It is farther removed from black, Jewish, and other minority locations. It is geographically remote and would require a much greater effort to uproot those entrenched there. It has more "wide open spaces" than probably any other area of the country and appeals to those who believe they have the right to hunt, fish, etc., without government regulation and licensing. It offers access to seaports and a way into Canada. Generally, this would be logical part of the country for such groups to covet.

THEOLOGICAL BASIS FOR RACIST BELIEFS

Identity theory teaches that the United States, not Israel, is God's promised land, and that non-white races were created before God created Adam. They believe that Jews are not the chosen people and their unjust claim to be the chosen people is only part of the international conspiracy to rule the world. They believe that at the coming of the Apocalypse, the earth will be rid of all except the Aryans and that this Armageddon will be coming soon. They believe that the final battle will occur in the cornfields of the Midwest instead of Israel.

Neo-Nazi doctrine conficts with this in that the neo-Nazis declare that the Israelites are ancestors of the Jews and the source of all evil, but they have not let this conflict keep them from supporting the Christian Identity movement and coordinating their efforts with this movement. Neo-Nazis have more attraction to Norse religions and Gods than with any recognized religious movement. The common thread is hatred of Jews.

Adherents of the Posse Comitatus doctrine also have a different emphasis at times, with their focus on legal technicalities and warning of collapse through economic forces or nuclear war rather than an apocalypse. Christian Identity theology provides a way to attract religious people to a racist movement and provides the racist movement with a theological excuse for their actions. The Posse Comitatus is connected to the overall Christian Identity movement, but has some definite ideas of their own.

The new citizen militias are, by and large, made up of those with connections to God and country. There are no religious beliefs specific to the "militia movement" but the belief in God and protecting one's constitutional rights and protecting their nation in whatever way they believe it needs protection is central to their beliefs.

SOPHISTICATED COMMUNICATIONS
Even before the Order wreaked havoc around the country, the 1983 Aryan Nations Congress made plans for a nationwide secure computer system to allow extremists from various groups to communicate. Louis Beam, of the Texas KKK and Aryan Nations, has created at least a dozen of thse bulletin borads and there are other creators of these communications systems also. These bulletin boards are used for anything from distributing a death sentence to ZOG representatives, to providing hate messages, recruiting new members, to allowing higher echelon

members to send coded messages to each other. These computer bulletin boards are inexpensive and virtually unregulated, both popular features with the right wing extremists.

The computer bulletin board systems have been kept "hot" in recent years after the Randy Weaver incident, Waco, and now the Oklahoma City bombing. Computer bulletin boards have often sent "recipes" for making bombs and other sophisticated information over the screen. Members of some of the newer militias have claimed to have broken into the government's electronic intelligence network.

Public access television is another way that the right wing extremist movement has accessed to spread their messages. They use their rights of free speech and freedom of religion to put their views before the public eye and ear. Tom Metzger is the dean of such usage.

Radio talk shows have become a radical medium for various right wing talk shows hosts. President Clinton has accused them of pushing people over the edge who already have radical ideas and only need a cause and a medium to take violent action. He was involved in accusations back and forth with the various hosts about them encouraging violent actions and him invading their freedom of speech by accusing them of being responsible for disasters.

Extremist groups keep the Internet busy with anti-government conspiracy messages and far right radio talk shows are heard by thousands. Francisco Martin Duran, the man arrested in October 1994 after firing many shots at the White House, reportedly listened to a talk show where the host made the sounds of a firing gun when talking about Congress and the federal government. The National Rifle Association (NRA) ran an advertisement in March 1995 likening agents of the BATF to "stormtroopers." This was echoed by Rep. John Dingell, D-Michigan, during House debate of the crime bill, calling them "jack-booted American fascists" with "no concern over the rights of ordinary citizens or their property" (*Southern Illinoisan*, 4/25/95).

Clinton was promptly counterattacked by many conservative talk-show hosts for his criticism of their rights of freedom of speech, and using this criticism to gain points against the right wing by using the tragedy in Oklahoma City. Their rhetoric is nothing compared to that of some of the right wing extremist network presentations and lately, even some militias. Mark Koernke was kicked off his weekly shortwave broadcast after putting forth some of his theories in the wake of the Oklahoma City bombings.

Right wing extremists are also using some more traditional methods of electronic contact to send their message along. Audio cassettes and video cassettes are available with messages from the leaders and can be listened to or watched at home. Mark Koernke was also active here and audio and videotapes have been distributed all over the country with his extremist militia views. Telephone "hot lines" have also been recently utilized for recorded hate messages.

PARAMILITARY AND SURVIVALIST TRAINING

Paramilitary and survivalist training is necessary to prepare for the battle of Armageddon and includes the gathering of intelligence information about enemies of the "cause." This training is a central tenet of the Christian Identity and Posse movements.

Most of the primary groups have established their own training sites and trainers. William Pierce moved to West Virginia and set up shop in an isolated area there. The Covenant, the Sword, and the Arm of the Lord (CSA) has traditionally pursued this paramilitary stance and has even given workshops to the general public for a fee (Coates, 1987). The Christian Patriots Defense League sponsored paramilitary training workshops for several years in Illinois, Missouri, and West Virginia (Coates, 1987).

The Aryan Nations have always had their own "security chief" responsible for training and on-site security (Martinez and Guinther, 1988). The Posse Comitatus is much more secretive about their training in that their doctrine requires that they keep their affiliations secret. That same doctrine requires them to stockpile weapons and food.

CONCLUSIONS

Information about right wing extremists is not available without an extensive search. Such extremists have not been the focus of research in the past as the threat to national security was always seen as coming from outside the country's borders. Incidents in the 1980's and 1990's have shown that the threat may indeed come from within and may be a greater threat than has been faced because of outside intruders. The American people have become upset with what they see as unneeded government interference and have looked for ways to take action. Sometimes they may become involved with groups and individuals they would not normally have approved of or become involved with because they have not found other methods that were responsive to their grievances. When Vicki Weaver talked of the "sounds of approaching thunder" it might have been a good time to go break out the umbrella or at least invite everyone to come in out of the rain and talk things over over a cup of coffee.

Violent incidents attributed to right wing extremists have increased dramatically during the past quarter of a century and the violent incidents have been of a different character than those seen previously. This violence has been aimed not only at the more traditional targets of such groups, blacks and Jewish, but also against the U. S. government and has included a conspiracy to overthrow the United States government, the first organized conspiracy by right wing extremists in this century. It has also included the largest mass murder in United States history, with the bombing of the Alfred P. Murrah Federal Building in Oklahoma City.

Looking at the historical backgrounds of some of the more violent and extreme groups and individuals, several of them had their beginnings with the more benign and less violent groups. There are also honest Americans who believe they are protecting their Constitutional rights who get involved in extremist movements. The more violent and extreme have kept pursuing a higher level of violence and coming up with more ways that more people are constricting their freedoms. They have no sorrow about the victims of the Oklahoma City bombing believing it was an acceptable retaliation for the women and children killed at Waco when law enforcement tried to end the standoff.

Changes are seen in the victims targeted by these groups, and much change is seen in the fellowship that has been created between those that would have previously been strange bedfellows. Neo-Nazis, whose ideology conflicts with Christian Identity doctrine, are a prime example. How these two groups can pursue a common goal and the latter group retain their Christian emphasis, is questionable, unless they believe the end justifies the means. Looking at these groups and individuals historically allows insight into how they justify their actions.

Conspiracy among the various groups and individuals appears to be on a much higher level and much more common than previously. A major effort at collaboration came in 1983 at the Aryan Nations World Congress, and much of the violence subsequent to that meeting may have connections to that meeting or have been planned there.

It was after this meeting that the Order came into being and a nationwide computer system was agreed upon to keep various groups in contact with each other. And, it was after this meeting that the conspiratorial efforts seemed to gather momentum.

The level of violence had increased as the 1980's approached, and after the groups began conspiring and created special groups such as the Order, and then the Bruder Schweigen Strike Force II, the violence was more coordinated and purposeful. Even though these groups were intercepted by authorities, evidence in their possession indicated they had had plans on a much grander scale, with terroristic activities that would endanger entire cities. Some members of the Order were never identified and continued operating as secret cells of the Order after the Order was defeated.

The idea of establishing one nation under the Aryan God is central to the several types of organizations researched. The right wing extremists do not make a secret of their desire to secede from the Union, create their own nation, and exile all non-Aryans to various sections of the country away from the Aryans. The Order was the primary well publicized effort to bankroll this new nation, but several of the groups have expressed their desire to create this nation by other means.

Even though there are differing ideologies among the various groups, they have come together around the idea that the world, as we know it, is going to end, and the Aryans must be prepared to take over their own nation when the apocalypse comes.

Christian Identity followers believe that this will be the time of Armageddon, the Posse believes that it will happen due to economic and nuclear threats, and the neo-Nazis believe that the Jewish will cause the world to collapse. These groups have been able to synchronize their ideas sufficiently to cooperate with each other, however.

The groups and their leaders have become sophisticated and have taken advantage of technological advances in communications. In using computer bulletin boards, they are using means of communication that are fairly unregulated, are very readily available, and offer various levels of security. This communication was not widely available at the time of the Order and might have had some effect on their level of efficiency had they had that advantage. Other publicly accessed communications such as videos, cable television, and even telephone hotlines have made their message much more accessible to the general public.

Many of the various types of groups are involved in paramilitary and survivalist training. Several of the groups, when authorities have had cause to take action against them, have had caches of illegal weapons, explosives, and even poison.

It is necessary to look at all these factors in their totality in understanding why such individuals and groups should be studied and their level of danger to this country assessed. It is not because such groups have differing religious and political views. It is only when such groups and individuals become involved in activities that are unlawful and harmful to the groups they target.

Perhaps one way to dispel some of the conspiracy theories the groups believe the government is engaged in, is to make the information more public. Many of the groups are not yet involved in the extreme fringe, but could be. Many of them are citizens who feel they have been wronged by their government and are buying in to ideas that the government is the enemy and they may have to take violent action to protect their rights. Maybe it is time to publicly acknowledge the conspiracy theories and show the citizens of the United States why there are Russian tanks on American soil, why bar codes are on road signs and embedded in currency, and why there are "black helicopters." Some of these have nothing to do with national defense and security and might allow the more sensible to realize that these things are not part of a nationwide conspiracy to take our guns, although it will not sway the diehards.

Reviewing the various factors listed shows that a change has occurred in the past two and one-half decades, and that change is toward a much more dangerous threat from right wing extremist groups and individuals. They have grown more violent, gathered together to conspire, shown their interest in establishing a separate nation at whatever cost to the remainder of the nation, and used their theology to recruit new members and justify their actions to the country at large. They have been active in paramilitary training that would allow them to carry forth their aims, and created more sophisticated means of communication than is available on a nationwide basis to most law enforcement authorities.

The recent advent of citizen militias has called attention to the right wing movement because people who would not normally be involved in the right wing are joining citizen militias that are oriented to the right. Citizen militia adherents have been linked to the Oklahoma City bombing and militia members are currently involved in standoffs with police attempting to arrest them in Montana.

All of these are reasons for studying these groups and individuals. Studying these groups can provide information for law enforcement authorities and others as to the operation, character, and dynamics of such groups and individuals. It may lend some insight as to how to approach them without creating more violence.

In the past, extremists have not been given much attention until a Gordon Kahl, Bob Mathews, Randy Weaver, or David Koresh came along. It is necessary that law enforcement coordinate their intelligence efforts and training in the same manner as the right wing extremists coordinate theirs and take these groups and individuals seriously.

Traditionally there has been conflict between federal law enforcement officers and local policemen and deputies. Because of the several disasters previously detailed, it is clear that all available information must be gathered and used before decisions can be made. Local authorities often have a better feel for the potential for violence and may have suggestions on how to approach the situations, if they are asked.

The recent incidents have been a black eye for law enforcement everywhere and particularly for federal officers. It has been demoralizing for the honest and competent officers who do things properly. When situations are handled badly, then those responsible need to be held responsible and policies changed in order that the situations be handled differently the next time.

The typology used shows how each type of individual fits into his niche in the group. Some individuals get involved with groups that are not only right wing, but violent, extreme, and criminal because these organizations meet their needs. This typology might be further expanded to develop a particular profile of individuals in each classification and provide a way to eliminate from scrutiny those right wing individuals and groups who are lawfully exercising their political rights. Whatever the reaction to right wing groups, it is clear that they have gotten the attention of the nation, and decisions must be made about what that means to law enforcement and the general public.

WORKS CITED

"America Has Long History of Revolt." AP story in *Southern Illinoisian*, Carbondale, Illinois, June 11, 1995, 9a.

Anderson, J. And J. Spears. "High Tech Network for Extremists." *The Washington Post*, November 4, 1986, E19.

Anti-Defamation League of B'nai B'rith. *The Identity Churches: A Theology of Hate*. New York: Anti-Defamation League of B'nai B'rith, 1983.

ADL. *Computerized Networks of Hate*. New York: ADL, January 1985 (1985a).

ADL. *Propaganda of the Deed*. New York, ADL, 1985b.

ADL. *The Populist Party*. New York, ADL, Fall, 1985 (1985c).

ADL. *Extremism Targets the Prisons*. New York: ADL, June 1986.

ADL. *Special Edition: William Pierce and the Neo-Nazi Church*. New York: ADL, February 1987 (1987a).

ADL. *The "Pace Amendment."* New York: ADL, May 1987 (1987b).

ADL. *The Committee of the States*. New York: ADL, October 1987 (1987c).

ADL. *Shaved for Battle: Skinheads Target America's Youth*. New York: ADL, November 1987 (1987d).

ADL. *Hate Groups in America: A Record of Bigotry and Violence*. New York: ADL, 1988a.

ADL. *Extremism on the Right*. (New York: ADL, 1988b).

ADL. *Special Edition: Tom Metzger*. New York: ADL, February 1989).

ADL. *Special Report: Neo-Nazi Skinheads, a 1990 Status Report*. New York: ADL, June 1990.

ADL. *Special Report: KKK Today*. New York, ADL, 1991a.

ADL. *Special Edition: Thom Robb, the Klansmen's New Clothes*. New York: ADL, October 1991 (1991b).

ADL. *Special Report: Sounds of Hate, Neo-Nazi Rock Music from Germany*. New York: ADL, 1992.

Bayles, Fred and David Foster. "Conspiracy Theories in Oklahoma City Bombing Developed Fast and Thick." AP writers in Marion Daily Republican, Marion, IL, May 8, 1995, 8.

Bellafante, Ginia. "Waco: the Flame Still Burns." *Time*, May 1, 1995, 47.

Best, Kathleen. "Terror in Oklahoma City: Suspect Lived in Area Noted for Anti-Government Zealots." *St. Louis Post Dispatch*, April 26, 1995, 7a.

Bishop, K. "Plot Against U. S. Described in Court." *New York Times*, February 28, 1988, 25.

Brown, Robert K. "The G-Man Returns Fire." *Soldier of Fortune Magazine*, October 1995, 72-75, 111-113.

Bryant v. Zimmerman. 278 U. S. 63 (1928).

Burden, O. P. "Peacekeeping and the Thin Blue Line." *Police Chief*, V. 59, June 1992, 16-18+.

Center for Democratic Renewal. *Background Report on Racist and Far-Right Organizing in the Pacific Northwest.* Atlanta, GA: Author, 1988.

Chalmers, D. M. *Hooded Americanism: The History of the Ku Klux Klan.* New York: Franklin Watts, Inc., 1981.

Chicago Tribune. "Former Posse Comitatus Land Auctioned for Taxes." AP story from Tigerton Dells, Wisconsin, August 30, 1993, 3.

Church, George J. "A Two-Bit Conspiracy." *Time*, August 21, 1995, 22-26.

Coates, J. *Armed and Dangerous: The Rise of the Survivalist Right.* New York: Hill and Wang, 1987.

Cook, Fred J. *The Ku Klux Klan: America's Recurring Nightmare.* New York: Julian Messmer, 1981.

Cook, J. G. *The Segregationists: A Penetrating Study of the Men and the Organizations Active in the South's Fight Against Integration.* New York: Appleton-Century-Crofts, 1962.

Coplon, J. "Skinhead Nation." *Rolling Stone*, December 1988, 55-65, 94.

Corcoran, J. *Bitter Harvest: Gordon Kahl and the Posse Comitatus.* New York: Viking, 1990.

Cosmotheist Church. An undated handout on the letterhead of the Cosmotheist Community, Arlington, Virginia, with the closing name of William L. Pierce.

C-Span. Satellite television coverage of Congressional hearings of the Randy Weaver/Ruby Ridge incident on September 6, 1995.

Dale, Jerry. Personal interview with Jerry Dale, former Pocahontas County Sheriff and now Magistrate of that county, in Marlinton, West Virginia, July 6, 1995.

Dale, Jerry. Phone interview, September 25, 1995.

"Day One." ABC television, May 18, 1995.

Delta Press, Vol. 34B, Winter 1995.

Dominion Post, "Labeled a Neo-Nazi Terrorist, Pierce Says He's Only a Writer." April 14, 1991, 1d, 2d.

Donaldson, Sam. *Nightline*, September 6, 1995.

Dudman, R. *Men of the Far Right*. New York: Pyramid Publications, 1962.

Duffy, Brian, et al. "Terror in the Heartland: The End of Innocence." *U. S. News and World Report*, May 1, 1995, 34-50.

Encyclopedia of Associations, Vol. I, Part II, 24th Edition, 1990.

Epstein, B. R. and A. Forster. *The Radical Right*. New York: Random House, 1967.

Farley, Christopher John. "America's Bomb Culture." *Time*, May 8, 1995, 56.

Farley, Christopher John. "Patriot Games." *Time*, December 19, 1994, 48-49.

Finch, Phillip. *God, Guts, and Guns*. New York: Seaview-Putnam, 1983.

Flynn, K. and G. Gerhardt. *The Silent Brotherhood*. New York: Free Press, 1989.

Forster, A. and B. R. Epstein. *Danger on the Right*. New York: Random House, 1964.

Fury, Chris. *ABC Nightline*, September 5, 1995.

Garson, G. D. *Political Science Methods*. Boston: Holbrook Press, 1976.

George, John and Laird Wilcox. *Nazis, Communists, Klansmen, and Others on the Fringe: Political Extremism in America*. Buffalo, NY: Prometheus Books, 1992.

Gibbs, Nancy. "Oh, My God, They're Killing Themselves!" *Time*, May 3, 1993, 26-43.

Ginger, Ann F. *The Law, the Supreme Court, and the People's Rights.* Woodbury, NY: Barrons Educational Series, Inc., 1973.

Ginzburg, R. *100 Years of Lynchings.* Baltimore: Black Classics Press, 1988.

Gitlow v. New York. 268 US 652, 45 S Ct. 625, 69 L Ed 1138 (1925).

Gleick, Elizabeth. "Who Are They?" *Time*, May 1, 1995, 44-51.

Gleick, Elizabeth. "On the Trail." *Time*, May 8, 1995, 50-53.

Goldman, S. *Constitutional Law: Cases and Essays.* New York: Harper Collins, 1991.

Hall, Mimi. "Internet Getting Senate Scrutiny." *USA Today*, May 12,1995, 5A.

Hoffman. B. *Terrorism in the United States During 1985.* Santa Monica, CA: Rand Corporation, 1986.

Holleman, Joe. "Militia Members Predict Crackdown on Gun Owners." *St. Louis Post Dispatch*, April 24, 1995, 5b.

Howse, J. "Dateline: Coeur D'alene, Shadow over Paradise." *Macleans,* November 10, 1986, 8-11.

Jackson, David S. "On the Moderate Fringe." *Time*, June 26, 1995, 62.

Jews for the Preservation of Firearms Ownership (JPFO). Fact sheet entitled "Introduction," Milwaukee, WI. Received September 1995.

Johnson, James. Handout distributed by Johnson to various county officials before the alleged shootings in November 1994 in Williamson County, Illinois.

Jordan, P. "The Aryan Mountain Kingdom: A Fantasyland of White Supremacy." *Life*, November 1986, 22-28.

King, W. "Neo-Nazis Dream of a Racist State." *New York Times*, July 5, 1986, 14.

Koppel, Ted. "Waco: Firestorm." ABC Nightline, May 5, 1995.

Koppel, Ted. "North American Volunteer Militia." ABC Nightline, May 22, 1995.

Lacayo, Richard. "In the Grip of a Psychopath." *Time*, May 3, 1993, 34-35.

Lacayo, Richard. "A Moment of Silence." *Time*, May 8, 1995, 44-48.

Lambrecht, Bill. "Radical Right Has Articulate Spokesman." *Post Dispatch* (St. Louis, MO), April 26, 1995, 5b.

Lamczik, Dennis. "No Incidents at KKK Rally." *Marion Daily Republican* (Marion, IL), April 9, 1995, 1a.

Larson, Erik. "ATF Under Siege." *Time*, July 24, 1995, 20-29.

Larson, Erik. "How A Cascade of Errors Led ATF to Disaster at Waco." *Time*, July 24, 1995, 28-29.

Levinson, Arlene. "Have You Heard the One about the UN Invasion?" AP Story in *Southern Illinoisan*, Carbondale, IL, June 11, 1995, 1a, 9a.

Loh, Jules. "The Real Ku Klux Klan Is Dead, Buried." *Benton Evening News Weekend*. April 19, 1995, 3C.

Macdonald, Andrew. *The Turner Diaries*. Arlington, VA: National Vanguard Books, 1980.

Macdonald, Andrew. *Hunter*. Hillsboro, WV: National Vanguard Books, 1989.

Martinez, T. and J. Guinther. *Brotherhood of Murder*. New York: McGraw-Hill, 1988.

McGuire, John. "'27 Bombing at School Tore Lives, Town Apart." *Post Dispatch* (St. Louis, MO), April 29, 1995, 13b.

Meddis, Sam Vincent. "Agents: Survivalist Was the Ignition for Idaho Tragedy." *USA Today*, September 8, 1995, 2A.

Miller, Susan and Myron Stokes. "One Family's Nightmare." *Newsweek*, March 13, 1995, 27.

Monitor. "Neo-Nazi Youth Gang Activity Builds Up." April 1988, 6.

Monroe, Sylvester. "Today Los Angeles, Tomorrow. . ." *Time*, July 26, 1993, 49.

NAACP v. Alabama. 357 US 449, 78 S Ct. 1163, 2 L Ed2d 1488 (1958).

National Alliance. "Free Money." Hillsboro,WV. Undated flyer.

Newsweek. "High Tech Hatred." December 24, 1984, 20.

New York Times. September 21, 1985.

Nilus, S. A. *Protocols of the Learned Elders of Zion*. New York: Beckwith, 1920.

Noto v. United States, 367 U. S. 290 (1961).

Ostfing, R. N. "A Sinister Search for Identity." *Time*, October 20, 1986, 74.

Pearson, Phil. "Tensions, No Violence, at KKK Rally." *The Evening News* (Benton, IL), April 9, 1995, 1, 10.

Pearson, Phil. "KKK Rally Cramps County Sheriff's Budget." *The Evening News*, April 26, 1995, 1.

Pierce, William L. "The Roots of Civilization." Hillsboro, WV: National Vanguard Books, publication #580.

Pierce, William L. "Gun Control: Not What It Seems." Transcript from speech on American Dissident Voices, January 29, 1994.

Police Against the New World Order. *Operation Vampire Killer 2000: American Police Action Plan for Stopping World Government Rule*. Phoenix, AZ, 1992.

Poor, Tim. "Three Men Made Bombs as Early as '92, FBI Says." *Post Dispatch* (St. Louis), April 26, 1995, 4A.

Post Dispatch (St. Louis, MO). "Racist Book Popular Among Extremists." © story from *LA Times*, April 24, 1995, 5b.

Post Dispatch. "Clinton Assails Hate Radio." 25 April 1995, 1.

Post Dispatch. (St. Louis, MO: New York Times News Service story). "Officers Cautious on Montana Fugitive." 17 May 995, 4a.

Post Dispatch. "Man Suspected of Buying Plague Bacteria." May 17, 1995, 8a.

Pritt, Pamela. "Local White Supremacist Leader Denies Connection to Oklahoma Bombing." *The Pocahontas Times*, April 27, 1995, 2.

Pritt, Pamela. "Media Descends on Mill Point, Pierce Discontinues Interviews." *The Pocahontas Times*, May 4, 1995, 2.

Pritt, Pamela. "Man Arrested for Possessing Deadly Virus Possibly Linked to National Alliance." *The Pocahontas Times*, May 18, 1995, 2.

Prochnau, B. "The Twisted tale of a Human Slaughter." *The Washington Post*, May 13, 1986, c1,2.

Rainie, Harrison, et al. "Armageddon in Waco: the Final Days of D. Koresh." *U.S. News and World Report*, 3 May 1993, 25-34.

Rankin, Robert. "Hearing Preparations Refocus Attention on Waco." *(Copyrighted story for *Knight-Ridder Newspapers* in *Sunday Gazette Mail)*, Charleston, WV, July 9, 1995, 10a.

Reid, T. R. "Computers Becoming Nation's Bulletin Board." *The Washington Post*, July 19, 1985, A4.

Remesch-Allnut, K. "Cults: Organized, Armed, and Protected by the First Amendment." *Police Product News*, 29 October 1985, 29-32.

Reese, Charley. "The Best Protection Against Tyranny is the Right to Bear Arms." *Orlando Sentinel*, October 12, 1993, A8.

The Resister: The Official Publication of the Special Forces Underground. "New World Order: Combat Arms Survey." Vol. I, 1994, #2,1.

Ridgeway, J. *Blood in the Face.* New York: Thunder's Mouth Press, 1990.

Ross, Loretta J. "Anti-Abortionists and White Supremacists Make Common Cause." *The Progressive*, October 1994, 24-25.

Rotunda, R. D. *Constitutional Law.* St. Paul, MN: West Publishing Company, 1987.

Salholz, E. and M. Miller. "Curbing the Hatemongers: The Feds Crack Down." *Newsweek*, September 1988, 29.

Saye, A B. *American Constitutional Law: Text and Cases.* Columbus, OH: Charles E. Merrill Publishing Company, 1975.

Schenck v. United States. 249 US 47, 39 S Ct. 247, 63 L Ed 470 (1919).

Scigliano, E. "Aryan World Congress: America's Down Home Racists." *The Nation*, August 30, 1986, cover, 144-147.

Searls, Tom. "White Supremacist's Ascension Watched." *Sunday Gazette Mail*, Charleston, WV, July 16, 1995, 1a, 21a.

Shipp, B. *Murder at Broad River Bridge.* Atlanta: Peachtree Publishers Limited, 1981.

Shotgun News. April 10, 1990, 169.

Simpkin, Jay. "The War on Gun Ownership Still Goes on." *Guns and Ammo*, March 1994, 24-25.

Smith, C. J. "Rural Radical Right: Politics of Fear and Hatred Amidst the Farm Crisis." *New Era of Hate.* Atlanta, GA: Center for Democratic Renewal, June 1987, 20-23.

Smith, R. George. "Sex Suspect's Home Yields Guns." *Omaha World-Herald*, Septgember 18, 1991, 1.

Smolowe, Jill. "Enemies of the State." *Time*, 8 May 1995, 58-69.

Southern Illinoisan Newspaper (Carbondale, IL). "Klan, Opponents, Face Off in Texas." AP Story from Austin, Texas, January 17, 1993, 8a.

Southern Illinoisan Newspaper. "Clinton: 'Enraged Rhetoric' Making People Paranoid." Knight-Ridder Newspapers Story, April 25, 1995, 4A.

Southern Illinoisan Newspaper. "Michigan Militia Leaders Quit." AP Story, Traverse City, MI, April 30, 1995, 11a.

Southern Illinoisan Newspaper. "Denmark to Extradite American Neo-Nazi to Face German Trial." AP Story, Bonn, Germany, May 9, 1995, 4c.

Southern Illinoisan Newspaper. "Agents Look Into Theft of Chemical Used in Bombing." Associated Press Story, Dupo, IL, 17 May 1995, 1.

Southern Illinoisan Newspaper. "Some Are Ready to Take Up Arms." AP Story from Noxon, MO, 6/11/95(A), 1D.

Southern Illinoisan Newspaper. "Messenger of Militias Draws a Crowd." AP Story from Twin Falls, ID, 6/11/95(B), 1D.

Southern Illinoisan Newspaper. "Militia Members Converge on Senate." News story from *Dallas Morning News*, Washington coverage, June 16, 1995, A1.

Strong, D. S. *Organized Anti-Semitism in America: The Rise of Group Prejudice During the Decade 1930-1940.* Washington, D. C.: Council on Public Affairs, 1941.

Suall, Irwin, et al. *Armed and Dangerous: Take Aim at the Federal Government.* New York: Anti-Defamation League,1994.

Suall, I. and D. Lowe. "The Hate Movement Today: A Chronicle of Violence and Disarray." *Terrorism*, Volume 10, N. 4, 345-364.

Sullivan, Christopher. "Racism: White Supremacists Seek Office." *Southern Illinoisan* (Carbondale, IL), June 10, 1990, c21.

Tharp, Mike. "Echoes of the Texas Tragedy." *U. S. News and World Report*, May 3, 1993, 33.

Tharp, Mike. "The Growing Militias: Thunder on the Far Right." *U. S. News and World Report*, May 1, 1995, 36.

Time. "Foiling a Revolt." May 4, 1987 (1987a), 24.
Time. "Free Speech: Part I." December 14, 1987 (1987b), 37.
Time. May 8, 1995, 35.
Time. May 8, 1995, 62-63.
Time. "The Next Militia Cause?" July 10, 1995, 16.
Time. "The Waco Hearings." July 31, 1995, 18.
Tucker, Richard K. *The Dragon and the Cross: The Rise and Fall of the Ku Klux Klan in Middle America.* Hamden, Connecticut: Archon Press, 1991.
Turner, J. and R. Williams, eds. *The KKK: A History of Racism and Violence.* Montgomery, AL: Klanwatch, 1982.
USA Today. "Terrorism's Innocent Victims." May 12, 1995, 4A.
VanBiema, David S. "When White Makes Right: Skinheads Carve Out Their Niche in American's Violent Culture of Hate." *Time,* August 9, 1993, 40-42.
VanBiema, David S. "The Message from Mark." *Time,* June 26, 1995, 56-62.
Vaughn, Doug. "Terror on the Right: The Nazi and Klan Resurgence." *Utne Reader,* August/September 1985, 44-57.
Wade, W. C. *The Fiery Cross: The Ku Klux Klan in America.* New York: Simon and Schuster, 1987.
Washington Post. January 13, 1987, A7.
Weiss, Philip. "Outcasts Digging in for the Apocalypse." *Time,* May 1, 1995, 48.
Whitney v. California (1927).
Williams, Hubert. "Terrorism and Local Police." *Terrorism,* Vol. 8, #4, 1986.
Woolf, Tom. "Political Agenda: Unseat Liberal Politicians." *Southern Illinoisan Newspaper,* April 30, 1995, 11a.
Worthington, Rogers. "From a Distance, Nebraska Nazi Agitates at Will." *Chicago Tribune,* January 4, 1994, 16, 19.
Yost, Pete. "The Siege at Ruby Ridge: FBI Shot to Kill His Wife, Weaver Says." AP story in the *Atlanta Journal/Constitution,* September 7, 1995, A4.
Zeskind, L. *The "Christian Identity" Movement: Analyzing Its Theological Rationalization for Racist and Anti-Semitic Violence.* Atlanta, GA: Center for Democratic Renewal, 1987, 1987a).

Zeskind, L. "Back to Barbarism: Hate Group Activity." *engage/social action forum-131*, June 1987 (1987b).

Zielenger, M. "Racists Mine Bible for Creed of Hate." *Charlotte Observer,* July 26, 1986, 1.

Zoglin, Richard. "All You Need Is Hate." *Time*, June 21, 1993, 63.

PHOTOS

#1 Knights of the Ku Klux Klan rally in Benton, IL, had Illinois and Indiana officials in attendance; photo courtesy of Benton Evening News

#2 Three Illinois state troopers with canines patrolled the enclosure that kept the Klan from the crowd, and vice versa; photo courtesy of Benton Evening News

#3 A crowd of several hundred were kept behind barricades; photo courtesy of Benton Evening News

#4 Illinois state troopers in riot gear patrolled the crowd; photo courtesy of Benton Evening News

#5 Not everyone in Benton, Illinois, was happy to see the Klan in town; photo courtesy of Benton Evening News

#6 Pocahontas County Courthouse, county seat of the county where the
National Alliance is located (photo by author)

#7 This "No Trespassing" sign is at the entrance of the road that leads to the National Alliance (photo by author)

#8 The National Alliance is accessed by traveling this long country lane to a padlocked gate that gives entrance to the mountaintop (photo by author)

#9 An aerial surveillance photo of the National Alliance compound on top of a West Virginia mountain (photo courtesy of Jerry Dale, former Pocahontas County Sheriff and now Magistrate)

#10 This large pole-barn structure housed the Cosmotheist Church at the National Alliance compound in West Virginia (photo courtesy of Jerry Dale)

#11 This mobile home structure is reportedly the residence of William Pierce, head of the National Alliance (photo courtesy of Jerry Dale)

#12 An aerial view shows another of the mobile homes on the mountaintop (photo courtesy of Jerry Dale)

APPENDIX A

JOHN BIRCH SOCIETY CONNECTIONS (People previously involved with the John Birch Society and their later affiliations).

Virgil Barnhill - American Rifle and Pistol Association/Florida Patriots

Willis Carto - Liberty Lobby/Populist Party/National Youth Alliance

Robert Bolivar DePugh - Minutemen/Committee of 10 Million

William Potter Gale - Posse Comitatus/California Rangers/Committee of the States

Ben Klassen - Church of the Creator

Robert Jay Mathews and Richard Scutari - the Order

Jack Mohr - Christian Emergency Defense System/Christian Patriots Defense League

William Pierce - National Alliance/Cosmotheist Church

Gerald L. K. Smith, Christian Nationalist Church

J. B. Stoner, National State's Rights Party

APPENDIX B
KU KLUX KLANS

The three primary Klans and their principals

United Klans of America
Robert Davidson/Calvin Craig
Robet Shelton
Louis Beam

Invisible Empire, Knights of the Ku Klux Klan
Bill Wilkinson, 1975-82
James Blair, 1982
James Farrands, 1986, Imperial Wizard
Roger Handley, Grand Dragon under Wilkinson

Knights of the Ku Klux Klan
David Duke (1974)
Don Black (1980)
Tom Metzger, California Knights of the KKK
Edward Fields/J. B.Stoner/New Order Knights of the KKK
Stanley McCollum
Louis Beam, Texas KKKK and Texas Emergency Reserve

Outline of the current Ku Klux Klans

1. United Klans of America, Inc. (UKA)
   A. Founded by Robert Davidson and Calvin Craig
   B. Began as Invisible Empire, United Klans, Knights of the Ku Klux Klan of America, Inc., shortened to UKA
   C. Organ is *The Fiery Cross*
   D. Headquarter is in Tuscaloosa, Alabama
   E. Robert Shelton, Imperial Wizard, 1961 when his Alabama Knights joined the UKA
2. Knights of the Ku Klux Klan
   A. Organ was *The Crusader*, changed to *The White Patriot*
   B. Tuscumbia, Alabama is headquarters
   C. David Duke was the leader in the 1970's, turned it over to Don Black
   D. Klan Youth Corps begun by David Duke
   E. Stanley McCollum leads the other faction of the KKKK with strong ties to Identity leaders
3. Invisible Empire, Knights of the Ku Klux Klan
   A. Organ is *The Klansman*
   B. Headquarters was Denham Springs, Louisiana, then moved to Shelton, Connecticut, then back south again
   C. Bill Wilkinson led the group from 1975-82; James Blair took over briefly
   D. James Farrands took over in 1986 due to Blair's ill health
4. California Knights of the KKK
   A. Independent order under Tom Metzger
   B. Formerly David Duke's organization
5. New Order, Knights of the KKK
   A. Begun by Edward R. Field and J. B. Stoner, who are anti-Black and anti-Semitic
   B. Associated with National States Rights Party
   C. Georgia organization
6. National States' Rights Party
   A. Absorbed Conservative Party, National White American Party, and North Carolina KKKK
   B. Organized by Stoner and Fields
   C. Hybrid of Klan and neo-Nazi organization

7. Tuscumbia-based Knights of the KKK
   A. Headed by Stanley McCollum of Tuscumbia, AL
   B. Strong ties to "Identity" leaders
   C. Organ is also called *The White Patriot*
8. Northwest Knights of the KKK
   A. Led by Kim Badynski, formerly active in Chicago/Ed Novak is now in Chicago
   B. Located in Washington State
   C. Badynski also participates in Aryan Nations activities
   D. Associated with McCollum's KKKK
9. White Patriot Party
   A. Led by Glenn Miller of Angier, NC
   B. Became the Southern National Front with Cecil Cox in 1986
   C. Southern National Front planned to merge with Democratic National Front, led by Gary Gallo
   D. Miller entered federal witness protection program in 1987 after testifying at Fort Smith grand jury against other extremists
10. Christian Knights of the KKK
    A. Imperial Wizard is Virgil Griffin of Mt. Holly, NC
    B. Often march through racially disturbed areas
    C. Horace King, the Grand Dragon in SC, pled guilty to a charge involving 750 sticks of dynamite
11. White Camellia Knights of the KKK
    A. Grand Dragon Charles Lee
    B. Texas Klan's Louis Beam, Grand Dragon, indicted for seditious conspiracy and arrested in 1987 in Mexico, later acquitted
12. American Knights of the KKK
    A. Bill Albers of Modesto, CA, is leader
    B. Has been linked to Aryan Nations
13. National Knights of the KKK
    A. James Venable, Stone Mountain, GA
    B. Loose confederation of "splinter" groups
    C. Southern White Knight split from Venable's group because he was not militant enough
14. Fifth Era Klan

A. Robert Miles prmoted strategy of returning to secret organization of hard core militants dedicated to preserving white supremacy

B. New Klan emphasizing anti-Semitism and neo-Nazism in all countries traditionally white in modern times

APPENDIX C

KLAN MEMBERS AND OTHER RIGHT WING GROUPS CONNECTED TO THEM

Robert Shelton (UKA) - **Committee of 10 Million**
David Lane - the **Order**
Bill Wilkinson, IE, KKKK - **Robert Miles, Mountain Church**
Tom Metzger, CA, KKKK - **New Christian Crusade Church/White Student Union/White Aryan Resistance**
David Duke, KKKK - **White Aryan Resistance/National Association for the Advancement of White People (NAAWP)**
Don Black, KKKK - **neo-Nazi**
Edward R. Fields and J. B. Stoner, New Order Knights of the **KKK - National States' Rights Party**
Stanley McCollum (KKKK), Thom Robb, Kim Badynski (Chicago and Northwest KKKK), Louis Beam (Texas KKKK and UKA), and Bill Albers (American KKK) - **all associated with Richard Butler of the Aryan Nations**
Karl Hand, KKKK Grand Dragon for David Duke - **National Socialist Liberation Front**
Wesley Swift, KKK - **Christian Defense League, along with Richard Butler**

APPENDIX D

PREVIOUS ORGANIZATIONAL CONNECTIONS OF DAVID DUKE AND TOM METZGER

DAVID DUKE
David Duke incorporated KKKK in Louisiana in 1974
Previously with National Socialist White People's Party
National Association for the Advancement of White People
Led California Knights of the Ku Klux Klan
Lost CA KKKK to Tom Metzger

TOM METZGER
Tom Metzger took over CA KKKK
Founded White Aryan Resistance
White American Political Association
"Race and Reason" (cable TV)
New Christian Crusade Church minister
White Student Union/Aryan Youth Movement
Acquired money from the Order

APPENDIX E

LIST OF NEO-NAZI GROUPS, THEIR PRINCIPALS AND THEIR ASSOCIATIONS WITH OTHER GROUPS

America First Committee - published the *American Lancer*

American Nazi Party, Chicago, later became the National Socialist White People's Party, had connections to James K. Warner, Matt Koehl, and Ralph Forbes' Sword of Christ Church

American White Nationalist Party, Columbus, Ohio (their Post Office box was used for "Gentiles United for Zionist Aims")

Aryan Resistance Movement, Suring, Wisconsin

Aryan Youth Movement, Fallbrook, CA (the Metzgers)

Christian Nationalist Church, Gerald L. K. Smith

Cosmotheist Church, associated with William Pierce's National Alliance

EuroAmerican Alliance, Inc. - tiny neo-Nazi group publishes the *Talon* and *EuroAmerican Quarterly*

German-American National Political Action Committee (GANPAC), California

LaRoucheans- followers of Lyndon LaRouche; they really fit no category

Liberty Lobby - Willis Carto

National Alliance - William Pierce, Mill Point, WV; Pierce split with Matt Koehl in 1970 and began the National Alliance in 1974; formerly National Youth Alliance

National Democratic Front, Wshington Grove, MD - Gary Gallo, publishes the *Nationalist*, few members with a mailing list of more

National Democratic Policy Committee - Lyndon LaRouche

National Socialist League/World Service, San Diego, CA; publishes *NS Mobilizer* and *Race and Reason*

National Socialist Liberation Front, Metaire, LA - founded by Joseph Tomassi, who was killed; Donald Rust took over, then Karl Hand

National Socialist Movement (NSM) - Cincinnati, Ohio, merged with National Socialist Liberation Front in 1980's

National Socialist Party of America (NSPA) - founded by Frank Collins who went to prison on child sex charges; Harold Covington took over

National Socialist Vanguard - Dallas, OR, and Goldendale, WA - Dan Stewart, Fred Turner, and Rick Cooper

National Socialist White America Party - Pacific Palisades, CA

National Socialist White People's Party (NSWPP) - San Francisco

Splinter groups of NSWPP:

National White People's Party - Charles White, Ashville, NC

White Party of America - Karl Allen, Washington, DC

American Nazi Party - John Robert Bishop, Davenport, IA

National Sozialistische Deutsche-Arbeiter Partei-Ausland Organisation (National Socialist Worker's Party - Overseas Organization) - Gary Rex Lauck, Lincoln, Nebraska; Lauck was formerly with now defunct National Socialist Party of America

National States' Rights Party (see also with KKK) - Marietta, GA; renamed National Socialist White People's Party, 1968, then the New Order, New Berlin, Wisconsin; Matt Koehl ws a founder and sitll leaders the New Order

National White People's Party - Ashville, NC

National Youth Alliance - began as Youths for Wallace; under control of Willis Carto of the Liberty Lobby until 1970 when William Pierce split with him; progenitor of National Alliance

New Christian Crusade Church - James K. Warner, associated with National States' Rights Party

New Nation, USA (NNUSA) - Morongo Valley, CA

New Order, formerly National Socialist White People's Party, Arlington, VA; also formerly the American Nazi Party

Populist Party - political party founded by Willis Carto of the Liberty Lobby

Security Services Action Group - Westland, Michigan

Silver Shirts - 1930's - predominantly of American rather than German origin; founded by William Dudley Pelley and Henry Beach (cofounder of Posse)

Socialist National Aryan People's Party - Post Falls, Idaho - Keith Gilbert went to prison for welfare fraud; he was the leader

Southern National Front - hybrid of Klan and neo-Nazi group

White American Political Association - now called WAR

White Aryan Resistance (WAR), Fallbrook, CA

White Party of America

White Student Union (WSU) - Tom Metzger and John Metzger

World Service, San Diego, CA

APPENDIX F

SKINHEAD GROUPS DISCUSSED IN THE TEXT

American Front, Salem, OR

Atlantic City Skins

Bay Area Skinheads (BASH) - San Francisco

Berzerker - used by skinheads to refer to someone who gets drunk and kills people; refers to a skinhead rock band; and may refer to the skinhead group that David and Bryan Freeman were trying to form when they murdered their family in Pennsylvania

Chicago Area Skinheads (CASH) - headed by Clark Martell who attended meetings at Robert Miles' Mountain Church; has connections to Detroit Area Skinheads

Confederate Hammer Skins

Creative Violence - Chicago Heavy Metal group

Detroit Area Skinheads (DASH) - Dave Lozon

Doc Marten Stompers - named for the combat boots, NY

East Side White Pride - Portland, Oregon - connected with White Aryan Resistance in the murder of Ethiopian student, Mulutega Seraw

Final Solution - skinhead rock group

Fourth Reich Skinheads, CA, led by Christopher David Fisher, ties with WAR, and the Church of the Creator in Florida, in plot to bomb First African Methodist Church in Los Angeles

North Hammer Skins

Romantic Violence AKA Chicago Area Skinheads

Skinheads Against Racial Prejudice (SHARP) - clashes with racist skinhead groups

SS Action Group - Cincinnati, OH, also in neo-Nazi section

SS of America, GA, publishes the *War Axe*

White American Skinheads (WASH), Cincinnati, OH, connected to SS Action Group

APPENDIX G

CHRISTIAN IDENTITY GROUPS AND GROUPS WITH TIES
TO CHRISTIAN IDENTITY GROUPS (SOME OF THESE ARE
LOOSELY CONNECTED AND SOME MAY HAVE TIES TO
OTHER ORGANIZED GROUPS)

All Citizens Equal (ACE)
America's Covenant Church, Medford Oregon - Ben Williams/Ron Poch
Americans First Lobby
American Tax Movement
Arizona Patriots - Ty Hardin
Aryan Brotherhood, prison chapter - Richard Butler
Aryan Nations, Hayden Lake, ID, led by Richard Butler
Aryan Resistance Movement, Suring, Wisconsin
Blue Ridge Hunt Club
Bruder Schweigen (Silent Brotherhood)
Bruder Schweigen Strike Force II, Aryan Nations, David Dorr offshoot of Bruder Schweigen
Calvary Temple Bible Church
Cedar Cutters - another name for CSA
Central Arkansas Patriots, Little Rock, Arkansas
Christ Kingdom AKA Christian Posse Association
Christian America Advocates, Mooreland, OK, Robert Kleuser
Christian Conservative Churches of America (CCCA) - begun by Johnny Bob (John Robert) Harrell in 1959, similar to Christian Patriots Defense League
Christian Crusade Church - Billy James Hargis founded in 1970
Christian Defense League - Wesley Swift and Richard Butler; James K. Warner, Baton Rouge and Arabic, Louisiana
Christian Emergency Defense Fund - Jack Mohr
Christian Liberty Academy - Tigerton Dells, Wisconsin

Christian Patriots Defense League (CPDL) - umbrella group led by John R. (Johnny Bob) Harrell, formerly of Clay County, Illinois, near Flora, no longer in that area

Christian Posse Association (also known as Christ Kingdom)

Church of Christ, LaPorte, Colorado, Pete Peters, Pastor

Church of the Creator, Ben Klassen, Otto, North Carolina

Church of the Creator, Niceville, Florida

Church of Great Republic

Church of Israel, Schell City, Missouri - Dan Gayman, Pastor, formerly the Church of our Christian Heritage - had connections with the Order

Church of Jesus Christ-Christian - Richard Butler and the Aryan Nations religious branch

Church of Our Christian Heritage - now Church of Israel

Citizen's Committee Involved

Citizen's Councils of America - opposed racial integration

Citizen's Emergency Defense System - Jack Mohr, Mississippi

Citizen's Equal Rights Alliance (CERA), against Native American treaty rights

Citizens' Law Enforcement Research Committee

Colorado Committee of 10,000

Committee of the States or Committee of the States in Congress Assembled, closely connected to the Arizona Patriots and led by William Potter Gale of the Posse

Committee of 10 Million - DePugh offered lifetime membership for $5

Covenant, the Sword, and the Arm of the Lord (CSA) - Jim Ellison and Kerry Noble, Missouri-Arkansas border

Duck Clubs - patriot groups in the Midwest

Elohim City - Adair, OK, Robert Millar

Emancipation of our White Seed

Family Farm Preservation - Tigerton Dells, Wisconsin

Farmer's Financial Freedom Foundation (another name for the Posse)

Florida Patriots (Virgil Barnhill was a member)

Freemen (loose group with Posse connections)

Heritage Library, Velma, OK, Larry Humphries

His Crusade Against Corruption - 1986, founded as one-man operation by J. B. Stoner

Kingdom Seekers Ministry

Iowa Society for Concerned Citizens (connected with Posse)

LaPorte Church of Christ - Pete Peters - Robert Mathews, David Lane, and Robert and Sharon Merki of the Order attended

Life Science or Basic Bible Churches (Posse Comitatus churches)

Life Science Church, Tigerton Dells, Wisconsin, Minister Donald Minniescheske

Lord's Covenant Church or America's Promise - Sheldon Emry, Phoenix, Arizona

Manifest Sons of God - Eldon Purvis

Ministry of Christ Church, Mariposa, CA

Minnesota Patriots Council

MoArk Survival Camp, Licking, Missouri -CSA

Mountain Church of Jesus Christ, or Mountain Kirk, Cohoctah, Michigan - Robert Miles, now deceased

National Agricultural Party

National Agricultural and Press Association - published *Primrose and Cattleman's Gazette*

National Association to Keep and Bear Arms (NAKBA)

National Commodities and Barter Association (NCBA)

National Emancipation of our White Seed - several white supremacists were involved, including Dan Gayman and Richard Butler

National Federal Lands Conference - local land control activists

National Legal Research Program for White Prisoners, Suring, Wisconsin (Robert Miles and Richard Butler)

New Christian Crusade Church, Metaire, Louisiana, allied with Christian Defense League

New Harmony Christian Crusade, Mariposa, CA - George Udvary

North Texas Patriots

Northwest Territorial Imperative or White Christian Republic or 10% Solution or White American Bastion - names for white separatist desire to establish homeland in Pacific northwest

Our Heritage Protection Association
Our Saviors Church, Gainesville, Missouri
Populist Party - political arm of the Posse
Posse Comitatus - founded by Henry L. (Mike) Beach, a former "Silver Shirt" and retired Army Col. William Potter Gale
Republic v. Democracy- Christian Patriots organization led by Robert Wangrud of Oregon City, Oregon
Robb, Thom - minister in Aryan Nations and KKK adherent
Sagebrush Rebellion - land rights' group in western states
Seattle Duck Club- ultraconservative group whose members murdered a family, mistakenly believing they were Jewish and Communist
Sons of Liberty - founded by James K. Warner of the Christian Defense League; also group started in 1972 by Robert Mathews
Sword of Christ Church - Ralph Forbes (formerly of American Nazi Party with George Lincoln Rockwell)
United Citizens for Justice - cochaired by Chris Temple, key supporter of Bo Gritz, Populist Party candidate for President in 1992
U. S. Christian Posse Association - William Potter Gale, 1969
Zarepath-Horeb -CSA compound; early name for CSA

APPENDIX H

ARYAN NATIONS (INCLUDING RICHARD BUTLER AND THE CHURCH OF JESUS CHRIST-CHRISTIAN) AND GROUPS WITH TIES TO THEM

National Emancipation of our White Seed
Aryan Nations World Congresses
Christian Defense League
Jim Ellison/Kerry Noble (CSA)
Louis Beam, Texas KKKK
Thomas G. Harrelson, bank robber, "FBI's 10 Most Wanted List"
Robert Miles, Mountain Church
White Aryan Resistance
Stanley McCollum, Knights of the KKK
Kim Badynski, Chicago and NW Knights of the KKK
Bill Wilkinson, IE, KKKK
Bill Albers, American KKKK
Robert Mathews, Gary Yarbrough, Eugene Kinerk, Elden Cutler, and David Lane of the Order
Argan Brotherhood (prison chapter)

APPENDIX I

LIST OF MEMBERS
OF THE ORDER (SILENT BROTHERHOOD)
(*Denotes original member)

NAME/CODE NAME/ORGANIZATION

*Robert Mathews/Carlos/National Alliance
*Andy Barnhill/Mr. Closet/CSA
*Jean Craig/Rainey
*Zillah Craig
Elden (Bud) Cutler/Aryan Nations
*Randolph Duey/Luke
*Jimmy Dye/Mr.May/National Alliance
*Randall Paul Evans/Calvin/KKK
*Richie Kemp/Jolly or Hammer/National Alliance
Eugene Kinerk/Aryan Nations
Ronald King/Prussian II
*David Lane/Lone Wolf/Aryan Nations
*Ken Loff/Marbles
*Thomas Martinez/National Alliance
*Ardie McBrearty/Learned Professor/Posse Comitatus
*Robert Merki/Noah/Church of Christ
*Sharon Merki/Mother Goose or Mrs. God/Church of Christ
Mike Norris/National Alliance
Jackie Norton/Beanstalk
Charles Ostrout
*Denver D. Parmenter II/Sandals
*Bruce Carroll Pierce/Logan,Brigham, and17 other aliases
*Randall Rader/Field Marshall and Big Boy/CSA
Dennis and Mary Schleuter/Church of Christ
*Richard Scutari/Joshua or Mr. Black/CSA
*Frank Silva/California KKK
*Bill Soderquist/Cripple/National Alliance
*David Tate/Church of Israel/AN
*Gary Yarbrough/Yosemite Sam or Reds\Aryan Nations
*George Zaengle\Legs

APPENDIX J

WILLIAM POTTER GALE'S OTHER AFFILIATIONS AND POSSE COMITATUS CONNECTIONS WITH OTHER GROUPS

William Potter Gale
*Ministry of Christ Church
*California Rangers (1960)
*U.S. Christian Posse Association (1969)
*Christian Conservative Churches of America
*Committee of the States
*Committee of the States in Congress Assembled (Nevada)
*Arizona Patriots
*Identity churches

Posse Comitatus connections
*Beach was former Silver Shirt
*Jim Wickstrom, preacher and orator
*Gordon Kahl
*Iowa Society for Concerned Citizens
*Oregon Militia
*Freemen
*Life Science Churches

APPENDIX K

MILITIAS AND ASSOCIATED GROUPS
DISCUSSED IN THE TEXT

Almost Heaven - armed community of about thirty families in Kamiah, Idaho, organized by Bo Gritz

American Justice Federation - Linda Thompson, Indiannapolis attorney

Blue Ridge Hunt Club - James Roy Mullins

Citizens for the Reinstatement of Constitutional Government - Albert Esposito, Monroe, North Carolina

Colorado's Free Militia - John Schlosser, claims 3000 members

Constitution Defense Militia - New Hampshire, Edward Brown

51st Missouri Militia - Ray Sheil, public informaton officer, named for the 51-day Waco siege

1st Regular Florida State Militia

Florida Militias (operate in various counties in Florida)

Gate Keepers - Pam Beesley, Kansas City, Missouri, information service

Guardians of American Liberties - Stewart Webb, Boulder, Colorado

Hillsborough County Dragoons, New Hampshire

Militia of Michigan or Michigan Militia Corps - organized April 1994 by Norman Olson and Ray Southwell, reportedly had connections to Mark Koernke, Tim McVeigh and James Douglas and Terry Lynn Nichols

Militia of Montana - most extreme of the militias discussed - headquartered in Cabinet Mountains near Noxon, Montana, John Trochmann, cofounder

North American Volunteer Militia - headquartered in Indiana; Montana coordinator is Calvin Greenup of Ravalli County, where Sheriff Jay Printz is involved in a standoff trying to arrest Greenup without violence

North Texas Constitutional Militia - honors Waco

Oregon Militia (organized long before the current militias)

Pennsylvania Militia - F. Co. of 9th Regiment

Placer County Unit of the California Unorganized Militia

Police Against the New World Order - Jack McLamb, Phoenix, Arizona

Texas Constitutional Militia - Jon Roland leads it; first muster was held on April 19, 1994, claims e-mail network and to have penetrated government electronic intelligence

Texas Emergency Reserve - fully armed militia type operation in late 1970's to early 1980's by Louis Beam

United States Militia - Key Largo, Florida

United States Militia Association - Samuel Sherwood of Blackfoot, Idaho

APPENDIX L

PUBLICATIONS PAST
AND PRESENT OF VARIOUS GROUPS

Action, now *National Alliance Bulletin* - National Alliance
American Covenant Newsletter - American Covenant Church
America's Promise - Lord's Covenant Church
American Mercury - early right wing magazine, bought by Willis
Carto and combined with other publications
American Party Newsletter - Chicago, IL
Armed Citizens News - National Association to Keep and Bear
Arms (NAKBA)
ANP Newsletter - American Nazi Party (1982)
Arizona Patriot - Arizona Patriots
Aryan Nations Newsletter - Hayden Lake, ID, Aryan Nations
Aryans Awake! - SS Action Group, Dearborn Heights, MI
Attack! - now called National Vanguard - National Alliance
Behold! - Republic v. Democracy - Oregon City, OR, Editor
Ed Arlt of the Aryan Nations
Blue Book of the John Birch Society
Calling our Nation - Aryan Nations
CDL Report - Christian Defense League
Christian America Advocate - Christian America Advocates,
Mooreland,
Christian Patriot Crusader - Jack Mohr, Bay St. Louis, Missouri
Christian Vanguard, Metairie, Louisiana, CDL
Citizen's Claw - Morongo Valley, CA, New Nation, USA
Crusader - formerly by David Duke, organ of KKKK in
Tuscumbia, now called the White Patriot
CSA Journal
Duck Club Magazine - fund raising idea to raise $10 million to
finance conservative campaigns
EuroAmerican Quarterly, EuroAmerican Alliance, Milwaukee,
WI
Fiery Cross, United Klans of America

Firearms Sentinel - Jews for the Preservation of Firearms Ownership

From the Moutain - Robert Miles' Mountain Church, Cohoctah, MI

GANPAC Brief - German-American National Political Action Committee, Santa Monica, CA

Good News America - Ralph Forbes, Sword of Christ Ministry

Groundhog - underground military newsletter

Hunter - Andrew Macdonald AKA William Pierce's book

Identity - Ministry of Christ Church, Mariposa, CA

Inter-Klan Newsletter - edited by Louis Beam and formerly Robert Miles, to pave way for Fifth Era Klan

Klansman - Invisible Empire, Knights of the KKK

Liberty Bell, Reedy, WV - no organization

Liberty Lowdown - Willis Carto's early publication

Liberty Net - nationwide computer bulletin board

Michigan Briefing - SS Action Group, Detroit, MI

NAAWP News

National Alliance Bulletin

National Socialist World - National Socialist White People's Party

National Spotlight - changed to *Spotlight*

National Vanguard, formerly called *Attack!*, publication of William Pierce's National Alliance

New Order - publication of former National Socialist Party of America, which became the New Order

NS Bulletin - New Order

NS Kampfruf - NDSAP-AO, Lincoln, Nebraska

NS Mobilizer - World Service, San Diego, CA

NSV Report - National Socialist Vanguard, Salinas, CA

NSWAP - National Socialist White American Party - Pacific Palisades, California

On Target - Minutemen

Operation Vampire Killer 2000 - Police Against the New World Order

Pathfinder - Christ's Gospel Fellowship - Spokane, WA

Paul Revere Club - Christian Patriots Defense League

Posse Noose - Jim Wickstrom

Public Voice - American Nazi Party of Chicago (1982)
Race and Nation - World Service, San Diego, CA
Race and Reason - Metzger's cable television program
Racial Loyalty - Church of the Creator, Otto, NC
Resister - Official Publication of the Special Forces Underground
Right - 1955-60 by Willis Carto
Rockwell Report - former publication of American Nazi Party
Scriptures for America - LaPorte, CO, Church of Christ
Spotlight - Liberty Lobby, Washington, DC
SS Action Group Michigan Briefing
Stormtrooper - former Amerian Nazi Party
Taking Aim - John Trochmann, Michigan Militia
Talon - EuroAmerican Alliance
Thunderbolt - National States' Rights Party
Turner Diaries - William Pierce AKA Andrew Macdonald
Truth at Last - Edward Fields changed Thunderbolt to this
WAR - Fallbrook, CA
Warrior World - Suring, Wisconsin, ARM
Washington Observer - earlier publication of Willis Carto
Watchman, Schell City, Missouri, Church of Israel
The Way - Hayden Lake, ID, Aryan Nations
Western Destiny - early publication of Willis Carto
White Aryan Resistance - WAR
White Patriot - Tuscumbia, AL, Knights of the KKK
White Power - the New Order
White Unity - American White Nationalist Party, formerly called the White Nationalist
World Economic Review - Christian Defense League
Zion's Watchman - Church of Israel, Nevada, MO
Zionist Watch - Liberty Lobby, Washington, DC

INDEX

Koehl 53, 57-8, 67, 2131-4
Koernke 102, 103, 152, 153, 166, 178, 225
Koppel 110, 127, 187
Koresh 7, 19, 27, 107, 135--140, 159, 172, 182, 189
Krause 102
Lacayo 102, 103, 120-122, 137, 153, 154, 188
Lambrecht 59-61, 63, 188
Lamczik 49, 188
Lane 85, 93, 145, 169, 201, 211, 219, 221, 222
LaRouche 70, 71, 213
Larson 138, 188
Lauck 68, 69, 214
leaderless cells ·82, 114
Lee 7, 54, 135, 209
Levinson 102, 188
Levitas 110
Liberty Letter 66, 67
Liberty Net 52, 113, 148, 149, 228
Liddy 12, 153
Life Science Church 90, 219
Lloyd 57
Loff 84, 87, 222
Loh 44, 188
Looker 109
Lord's Covenant Church 93, 219, 227
lynchings 44, 187
MacCrae 109
Macdonald 59, 60, 86, 127, 132, 154, 188, 228, 229
Mariposa 88, 92-3, 219, 228
Marlinton 61, 62, 186
Martell 74, 114, 216
McBrearty 85, 87, 222
McCabe v. Arave 4, 34
McCollum 48, 50, 207-209,

211, 221
McGarrity 84
McGiffen 49
McGuire 126, 188
McLamb 106, 131, 226
McVeigh 16, 25, 101, 103, 104, 120, 127-129, 152, 160, 225
Meddis 123, 188
Merki 85, 87, 93, 219, 222
Militia of Montana 6, 101, 105, 106, 225
Mill Point 58, 60, 62, 142, 189, 213
Miller 5, 52, 55, 66, 76, 87, 113, 133, 149, 157, 188, 190, 209
Ministry of Christ Church 88, 219, 224, 228
Mississippi Burning 35
Mohr 91, 92, 95, 206, 217, 218, 227
Monitor 34, 74, 109, 149, 171, 188
Monroe 95, 108, 132, 188, 225
Morierty 69
Mullins 109, 126, 225
Murphy 4, 33, 34, 49
Murphy v. Missouri Department of Corrections 4, 33, 34
Murrah Federal Building 101, 126, 129, 174, 179
NAACP v. Alabama 4, 32, 188
NAAWP 48, 211, 228
NAKBA 96, 219, 227
National Agricultural Press Association 97
National Commodities and